Robert Barnwell Roosevelt, Seth Green

Fish Hatching, and Fish Catching

Robert Barnwell Roosevelt, Seth Green

Fish Hatching, and Fish Catching

ISBN/EAN: 9783337163969

Printed in Europe, USA, Canada, Australia, Japan

Cover: Foto ©Lupo / pixelio.de

More available books at **www.hansebooks.com**

FISH HATCHING,

—AND—

FISH CATCHING.

—BY—

R. BARNWELL ROOSEVELT,

Commissioner of Fisheries of the State of New York, Author of Game Fish, etc., etc.,

AND

SETH GREEN,

Superintendent of Fisheries of the State of New York.

ROCHESTER, N. Y.:
UNION AND ADVERTISER CO.'S BOOK AND JOB PRINT.
1879.

FISH HATCHING.

INTRODUCTION.

During the few years which have intervened since the discovery of fish culture, its practice has advanced with rapid strides, and although it is still little more than in its infancy; the laws which govern its management have been so far ascertained and applied that it is now an established art, capable of yielding vast results for the benefit of mankind. The days of doubt and uncertainty have passed away, and numerous experiments leading invariably to the same end have established it on a firm basis. For a time cautious persons, even when most enthusiastic could not help questioning in their own minds what the final outcome would be, and whether all that was predicted for the new undertaking would be realized, but success in all well considered and properly conducted attempts has swept away fear and hesitation, and experience may now be said to have fully confirmed the highest hopes of the most sanguine. The possibilities which fish culture suggested were so far beyond what can be obtained in other fields of human labor, so greatly exceeded the best results in agriculture that it seemed impossible that they could be realized, or that this enterprise would have remained so long undiscovered or undeveloped. But day after day and year after year the theory has been put in practical operation, where all its steps could be and were accurately noted, and the incredible increase and profit obtained left but one conclusion possible. No persons could be more cautious, more slow to express a positive opinion, or to accept a hasty judgment than the authors of this work, as they can show by all their writings, acts and utterances, but they feel at last that they and the public can give perfect credence to the claims of fish culture, provided it be conducted as intelligently and wisely as other departments of modern human labor.

It must not, however, be forgotten that this new art is as exact and exacting as any other, nor that it has its limits and must be managed with care and not slurred over or slighted. To the ignorant and indifferent it will yield no more than the cultivation of the land and possibly not so much, and precisely what those limits are of which we speak and what are the requisites of circumstance and manipulation, this work is intended to show. This is meant for a practical book on a practical subject, in which nothing shall be stated on conjecture; no mere fancy picture however alluring shall be presented to the public, and the bare facts with plain directions shall be given that all who wish may read and understand, and all who have the opportunity may practice what is herein set forth. With that view no attempt will be made at grace of diction, and scientific names, formulas and information will be omitted as far as is thoroughly consonant with the purpose to be attained, and no farther. Many misapprehensions exist in the public mind in relation to a matter which has dawned upon the world so lately and so suddenly, expectations as extravagant in some directions as they are depressed in others, and while one man will try to raise the best of fish from the worst of waters, another doubts if anything can be achieved from the most favorable opportunities. It is the function of this book to correct these mistakes and prevent these blunders.

The culture of fish has been gradually extended from one species to another until we have a fair idea of what can be done in all cases, and those even who try new experiments have much to guide them, and can, up to a certain point tread with assured footsteps. At first the only species treated by the artificial method was the salmon, the most valuable and highly prized; thereafter the process was applied to trout, then to shad and afterward to whitefish, lake-trout, herring, perch, bass, striped bass, sturgeon and many others with more or less success. The greatest promise for purely artificial manipulation is with the salmon, the trout, the lake-trout and the shad, but the close study of the habits of other varieties which followed the attempts with them have so familiarized the fishculturists with the necesities of their growth and increase that a subsidiary branch of fish-culture has grown up in which the natural process is assisted, protected and developed. This incidental method has yielded benefits that,allowing for the difference of labor and money expended, approach those reached through the more scientific and intricate management of the higher classes of fish. All these processes will be considered, explained and fully detailed in order that the utmost benefit may be received by the reader from the knowedge acquired by more than twenty years of study and experiment in the production and growth of fish. We believe that we can safely say that the authors of this book have had a hundred fold more experience in pisciculture than any other persons in this country, and that by them, or under their control, the most important inventions and discoveries have been made, either in the best methods of impregnating and hatching the eggs, or in protecting, transporting and growing the fish. They have been practically engaged in fish culture since its introduction into America; have studied, labored, and experimented in all its departments: have tested all theories propounded abroad and at home, and have had under their charge in the New York state hatching house the largest and most efficient establishment in the world for producing actual results, and for separating fact from error. As a consequence they feel they can promise that nothing will be given as an established fact that has not been fully proved by the personal experience of the writers, for they are resolved to make this book trustworthy if it is nothing else.

Before entering upon the details of practical management, it may not be unadvisable to take a general review of fish culture, and give some suggestions of universal application. It has been said that an acre of water would produce as much as five acres of land, if it were tilled with equal intelligence. In making such a comparison, it must be borne in mind that the crop of one needs no manure, requires no care during its period of growth and after it has once been planted, and that it is harvested by simply taking it from the water in which it dwells. It is almost wholly profit. The other must not merely be planted but must be fertilized at great expense, and worked and cultivated with assiduous labor of man and beast, and finally when at last successfully harvested and saved from destruction through disease, insects and the elements, it yields but a meagre advance upon the cost of time and trouble. It has been the habit to cultivate the land and neglect the water, the one has been reduced to private ownership and constitutes a large part of individual wealth, while the other is a sort of common property too little appreciated to be reduced to possession where this is possible, and abandoned as a sort of waste to yield what it may without care to the few chance persons who make a living out of it. If our wheat crop is damaged or the corn crop diminished or the cotton crop short, the public press rings with lamentation, and the country mourns over a national calamity. But the supply of our fish crop yielding millions of pounds of food per annum may be in process of utter annihilation, and yet no voice is raised, and we sit by with folded hands in idleness. The land we value dearly, because to till it costs us dear in sweat and thought, and the water we despise because it yields its free will offering without an effort on our part. We have tilled the ground four thousand years, we have just begun to till the water.

KINDS OF WATER AND FISH–FECUNDITY–COLD-BLOODED CREATURES.—Fish can be raised with less trouble and cost than other articles of food. The lakes and rivers are full of animal and vegetable organizations upon which fish can live, now wasted, but which should be utilized by stocking these waters by suitable varieties. There is not only an abundance of food, but it is also true that fish need less food to produce a given amount of flesh than is required by birds or quadrupeds. The amount which will make a pound of poultry or beef, will make many pounds of fish; this is owing to the fact that they are cold blooded and usually inactive animals. When we see them in water, they are in motion because they see us; at times they go long distances in search of breeding places, but they are, as a rule, quite torpid in their habits. Animal action consumes the system. For this reason, those who wish to fatten cattle or poultry keep them confined. Animal heat is also a great consumer of food, and a large share of all that is eaten by warm blooded animals is needed to maintain this vital heat. As fish are cold-blooded, they need but little food for this purpose, and most that they take goes to make bulk and weight. The fact that this class of animals will live a long time without eating anything is familiar to all. There is but little waste of their system in any way. We frequently see birds and fishes kept in the same rooms, while the first are restless and need constant care and feeding, and frequent cleansing of their cages, the latter are almost motionless, unless disturbed; and as the water in which they are kept is usually clear and fresh, it has in it but little food.

It may be true that a pound of fish does not contain as much nourishment as a pound of beef, but the difference is by no means as great as the difference in the cost of production. For some purposes of health it is much more valuable than a like weight of other food. Less care and labor are needed to raise fish than to raise other animals, or even to raise vegetables. We must give close attention to our flocks and herds throughout the year, and we must toil through a long season in our fields to make vegetables grow. Lakes and rivers are well said to be like fields prepared for seed. Fish only need our help in one way. At breeding times their eggs are mostly destroyed by numerous enemies, and but few are hatched. By artificial means at a trifling cost nearly all the eggs can be saved, and vast numbers of young produced.

While on this analogy, it may be suggested that rotation of crops may be as advantageously introduced in piscicultute as in agriculture. In a portion of France, where the land is low and can be overflowed at pleasure, by a system of dyking, crops of grain and eels are alternated, the latter being the most profitable, but this is only the germ of the true principle. When one sort of root or grain or vegetable is repeated on the same land, it is found that the soil is exhausted of its food, while its enemies are augmented in number. Identically the same thing occurs with fish when they are kept in one locality. They use up their food and increase the list of their foes. So soon as this happens they suffer, and should be supplanted by a different species, living on different food, and having a totally different class of enemies. Wherever this has been done, the effect has been surprising, the new species increasing enormously for the first few years, and then meeting the fate of its predecessors. It is a curious fact that the stomachs of fish are so often found to be entirely empty of food, and the migratory varieties seem hardly to feed at all while preparing to spawn. This would imply either that they digest very rapidly, or can go a long time without nutriment, and, probably, both of these deductions are true. Heat and motion are the main consumers of food, for animal bodies are physically machines, which must be supplied with fuel if motion is to be generated, and will wear out with friction unless the waste is restored. A man or a horse can only perform his quota of work if his body is thoroughly nourished, and, on the other hand, neither needs nor can digest his full amount of food unless he works. The terrestrial animals are warm blooded and active, many of them, in their natural state, getting their food by the chase, whereas fish are cold blooded, and, although occasionally making long journeys, are ordinarily quiet.

The following points upon fish culture seem to be established: First—Fish culture, extending to every desirable variety of fish is entirely practicable. Second—It may, under proper management, be made profitable to the producer; as much so or more than the cultivation of land, or of land animals, and on similar conditions. Third—It may furnish to all classes an abumdance of cheap, and the most nutritious and healthful food.

Fourth—It is absolutely necessary in order to the preservation of the fish of the country from total destruction. Fifth—Every section of our country, and all its creeks, rivers, lakes and seacoasts are available for this, care being taken that the right kinds of fish be selected for the waters into which they are placed, observing latitude, climate, temperature and quality of the water. Sixth—It may be carried on by stocking waters with young fish brought from hatching establishments, or by obtaining eggs for hatching, and both eggs and young fish may be transported safely to almost any distance. Seventh—The money capital required for these operations is small, skill, care, patience, perseverence and common sense, the same as in any other business, being the chief requisites. Eighth—Individual enterprise is alone sufficient for success, though State action is desirable; indeed, legislation is essential, if not to foster at least to protect those engaged in the business of fish culture.

CHAPTER I.

FISH CULTURE.

We do not propose to trace back the science of fish culture to its origin, nor settle the disputed claims of individuals or nations, to its discovery. That the old stagnant, almond-eyed nation of the East may have known something of it, as that curious, half developed race had misty intimations of many other important natural phenomena is not to be doubted; but the knowledge was of small extent and little utility, and has remained like the people among whom it existed, without development. Its practice consisted mainly in transporting from place to place, certain varieties of fish-eggs, which had the peculiarity of sticking to whatever they touched after emission from the parent. These were caught on twigs, sticks, and branches of trees, and so carried wherever they were needed. They were protected as they developed, and used to stock waters which had been depopulated. This was but a rude attempt at fish culture, and beyond it there was little more real foundation than for the pretence of hatching spawn in the eggs of fowls beneath setting hens.

The children of Confucius, thousands of years ago, in this as in many other investigations, commenced groping from the darkness of ignorance toward the light of truth; but before they had passed into the twilight of the morning, they seemed to be stricken with paralysis, and like the fabled seven sleepers, have stood on the semblance of death ever since.

The French have the honor of originating fish culture as now practiced among civilized nations. Two Frenchmen, called Rémy and Géhin, having observed that the mature eggs of certain fish flow from their bodies on the slightest pressure, and comprehended what important results might be obtained by taking advantage of this peculiarity.

It was some years after these discoveries in France that America commenced to take an interest in this subject, and from its geographical conformation and political government, labored under the greatest disadvantages. Many different States have conflicting rights in the same waters. Rivers rising under one jurisdiction, frequently pass under several others before they reach the sea; lakes touch or are included within four or five States; streams divide or bound two or more sovereignties. This diversity of control, and often of interest, naturally threatened to be fatal to any attempt at fish culture which required a uniform system in all waters to which it is applied. Take as an example of this difficulty, the most southerly of all known American salmon rivers of the Atlantic coast - the Connecticut. This magnificent water-course, once abounding in countless myriads of the noblest of fish, rises amid the wild, rugged hills on the confines of Maine and Canada near the lakes in whose crystal waters still sport the largest brook trout of America. Concentrating its numerous tributaries into one grand river, it flows between the green mountains of Vermont and the still more imposing ranges of New Hampshire; next it cuts Massachusetts nearly in two, and finally sweeping through Connecticut, now deep enough to float vessels of war and carry important commerce, it empties into Long Island Sound. Here we have in the first place the rights and interests of the estuary fishing at its mouth, once valuable net fisheries for salmon, and still productive of shad; in these the State of Connecticut is deeply concerned. Above these are the dams at Holyoke, fatal to all migratory fish, among which are to be counted both the salmon and shad, but which have contributed much to the wealth of Massachusetts, and are busy all year long in driving millions of looms and spindles. Farther north, the residents along the fluvial portion of the stream, in Vermont and New Hampshire, complained that for more than half a century no salmon or shad has been permitted to reach them and to bring their welcome dowry of wholesome food to their very doors. While still further to the northward the lumbermen must be consulted as to what effect the introduction of salmon and shad culture will have on their rafts and rafting dams.

Our country has a compensation in the character of its fish which more than makes up for these disadvantages, and has led to a more vigorous prosecution of fish culture, and more valuable discoveries in implement and methods than in any other land. The fish of North America are the finest in the world for food and sport, while some species have peculiar recommendations to the fish culturist. Probably the most valuable variety to be found anywhere is the shad; it is scarcely surpassed for the table, it is among the most prolific, it is the most easily manipulated, its eggs hatch in the shortest time, its fry require no care after birth, and being migratory it draws its sustenance from the sea while it travels far inland, in its periodic visits to the land. We have abundant varieties for the vast extent of valuable waters in our states, from the sluggish turbid streams and ponds of the South to the lively sparkling spring brooks of the North; from the smallest ponds to the immense inland seas of fresh water. For the lakes, the Whitefish, Salmon Trout, Herring, Black Bass and Wall-eyed Pike; for the rivers, the Yellow Perch, Black Bass, Shad and Salmon; for still and deep streams, the Bullhead or Catfish, the Perch and many other kinds of coarse fish; for the swift mountain stream, the Trout, Gold Fish, a good coarse pan fish, can be grown in all our rivers and bays. Beyond doubt, with very little care and expense these fish can be made to abound in our waters. But for some kinds this requires government aid, since individuals owning parts of streams will not hatch out fish there at their own expense for the benefit of all other owners of the stream, and special legislation seems to be required to get fish-passes constructed over the numerous dams in our rivers and to prevent substances destructive to the fish being thrown into our streams, such as saw-dust and the refuse of paper mills, tanneries and dyeing establishments.

But if with comparatively little care and expense our great rivers can be stocked, in the meanwhile there is room enough for private enterprise. There are few farmers in our country who do not have upon their land a lake, or spring, or clear running stream. If these men knew how easily they could turn this water to profit, not only by raising food for themselves, but a supply for the city and village market, there would soon be very few waters without their finny inhabitants. How much this would add to the wealth of the country any one can see at a glance.

Fish culture is not a matter either wholly of public or private interest, in part it is one, in part the other. The great lakes, the immense rivers, the long line of ocean coast can only be restocked by governmental aid and for the general good, but the private ponds, the small streams and the individual fisheries are to be replenished by private effort, and for the special benefit of their owners. As the shad are probably the best and most valuable fish for the public, so is the trout wherever it belongs or can be acclimatized the most desirable for individual purposes. The shad yields the largest amount of food while the trout holds the highest price in market, and possesses as a subject of sport a still higher value. Where neither shad nor trout can live some variety of the fresh water bass will answer for private or public waters, and the pike perch, (wall-eyed pike) is admirably adapted to larger rivers and lakes. There is hardly any pond, stream, river or lake, be it large or small that cannot be utilized, and the land owner that has not the facilities for raising salmon may supply his family with an excellent article of food in the shape of bullheads or gold fish.

The number and kinds of fish that are treated are increasing daily. The chinese probably confined their efforts to carp. We began on salmon. Then the effort was extended to trout, then to shad, to salmon trout, to whitefish, to striped bass, to sturgeon, to smelt, to grayling and indirectly to black bass, strawberry bass, oswego bass, pike perch, yellow perch, catfish, oysters, lobsters, gold fish, and other fresh water fishes, and we may confidently expect in time, to assist nature in multiplying all or nearly all the fishes that live on our coast or in our lakes and rivers. Not a year passes but some new and valuable discovery is made, and the importance and interest of fish culture increases with every development. Already twenty four states and territories have appointed commissioners to protect and develop their fisheries while the United States have established a Fishery Commission for the entire Union. The systems followed in the United States and abroad, even in modern Europe are wholly different. The famous establishment at Hueninguen, which having been founded by France, came through the fortune of war under the dominion of Germany is conducted on a plan that seems to us less effective and more wasteful that is adopted here. There awards are offered for ripe fish, which are secured and kept alive by individuals in any part of the country, and information of the fact is sent to the authorities at Hueninguen, who dispatch an expert to take the roe and melt which are then hatched at that establishment under government care; the living fry being distributed again at government expense. In this operation there is more labor and less profit than there should be. There is danger of depleting the waters from which the eggs are taken, and while certain streams are replenished others may be impoverished. With us mature trout are kept for the express purpose of breeding, no shad, whitefish or salmon trout are used, except those that would be caught and killed by the fisherman, and salmon eggs are only obtained from rivers teeming with a supply. As for the New York commission we can say no fish are killed purposely to obtain their eggs, and no streams can possibly have been depleted by the action of the commission.

There are certain well marked eras in fish culture in which the main discoveries have been made. Most of the appliances adopted abroad have been abandoned with us, and great strides have been made in developing the art. Our first great discovery was what is known as dry impregnation, that is the use of little or no water in impregnating the eggs with the male fluid. This was kept a secret however, from the public until it was re-discovered in Russia. Here it was first practiced in 1864, and up to that time twenty-five per cent. of the eggs was the greatest number impregnated; immediately afterwards the proportion rose to seventy-five per cent. and is now ninety eight. At present "dry impregnation" is universally adopted. The next great discovery in appliances was the shad hatching box, which has never been superceded for certain classes of fishes and situations, nor has it been improved on since it was invented. Another seemingly trivial but extremely important discovery was the application of coal tar as a coating to wood work and all articles that come in contact with the eggs, and on which fungus could do harm by growing. The last was the invention of the Holton hatching box for hatching whitefish, but which is a valuable convenience in managing the eggs of all the salmon and trout. These discoveries have reduced the labor and expense of fishculture immensely, and have added in an equal degree to efficiency and certainty of success.

COMMISSIONERS OF FISHERIES—As the reader may desire to communicate with the commissioners of one or more of the states, we append a list of their names and addresses as they were in the year 1878:

UNITED STATES.
Prof. Spencer F. Baird,................. { Smithsonian Institute, Washington, D. C.

DOMINION OF CANADA.
W. F. Whitcher,..Ottawa.
W. H. Venning,...St. John.
    Inspector of Fisheries for New Brunswick and Nova Scotia.

MAINE.
E. M. Stilwell,...Bangor.
Henry O. Stanley,....................................Dixfield.

NEW HAMPSHIRE.
Samuel Webber.....................................Manchester.
Albina H. Powers,..................................Grantham.
Luther Hayes,..Milton.

VERMONT.
M. Goldsmith,..Rutland.
W. H. Lord, D. D.,..................................Montpelier.

MASSACHUSETTS.
Theodore Lyman,..................................Brookline.
E. A. Brackett......................................Winchester.
Asa French,...South Braintree.

CONNECTICUT.
William M. Hudson,................................Hartford.
Robert G. Pike,....................................Middletown.
James A. Bill,.....................................Lyme.

RHODE ISLAND.
Newton Dexter,....................................Providence.
Alfred A. Reed, Jr.,...............................Providence.
John H. Barden,...................................Scituate.

NEW YORK.
R. U. Sherman,....................Oneida Co., New Hartford.
Robert B. Roosevelt,.............................New York City.
Edward M. Smith,................................Rochester.

MICHIGAN.
Eli B. Miller,......................................Richland.
George H. Jetome,................................Niles.
Andrew J. Kellog,................................Allegan.

NEW JERSEY.
J. R. Shotwell..Rahway.
G. A. Anderson,..Trenton.
D. Howell,..Woodbury.

VIRGINIA.
A. Mosely,..Richmond.
Dr. W. B. Robertson,....................................Lynchburg.
W. G. Ellzey,...Blacksburg.

ALABAMA.
Charles S. G. Doster,...................................Montgomery.
Robert Tyler,...Montgomery.
D. R. Hundly,...Cortland.

CALIFORNIA.
B. B. Redding,..Sacramento.
S. R. Throckmorton,.....................................San Francisco.
J. D Farwell,...San Francisco.

PENNSYLVANIA.
H. J. Reeder,...Easton.
R. L. Hewitt,...Hollidaysburg.
J. Duffy,...Marietta.

OHIO.
John C. Fisher,...Coshocton.
John H. Klippart,.......................................Columbus.
Robert Cummings,..Toledo.

MARYLAND.
T. B. Ferguson,...Baltimore.
P. W. Downes,...Denton.

IOWA.
Sam B. Evans,...Ottumwa
B. F. Shaw..Anamosa.
Charles A. Haynes,......................................Waterloo

MINNESOTA.
R. O. Sweeny,...St. Paul.
Wm. Golcher,..St Paul.
Robert Ormsby,..

WISCONSIN.
Hon. Harrison Ludington,................................Milwaukee.
A. Palmer,..Boscobel.
William Welch,..Madison.
P. R. Hoy,..Racine,
H. F. Dousman,..Waterville,

ILLINOIS
W. A. Pratt, ... Elgin.

ARKANSAS.
N. H. Fish, ... Pine Bluffs.
J. R. Stulman, ... Little Rock.
N. B. Pearce, ... Fayetteville.

KENTUCKY.
Pach, Thomas, ... Louisville.
P. H. Darsey, ... Caldwall County.
Polk Laffom, ... Hopkins County.
S. W. Coombs, ... Warren County.
C. J. Walton, ... Hart County.
James B. Casey, ... Kenton County.
John A. Steele, ... Woodford County.
J. H. Bunce, ... Garrard County.
T. T. Garrard, ... Clay County.
W. C. Allen, ... Bath County.

UTAH TERRITOY.
A. P. Rockwood, ... Salt Lake City.

WEST VIRGINIA.
John W. Harris, ... Louisberg.
Henry B. Miller, ... Romney.
C. S. White, ... Romney.

CHAPTER II.

TROUT CULTURE.

GENERAL CONSIDERATIONS.

There are but few salmon rivers in this country. This may be changed by the introduction of the California salmon, which will endure a higher temperature than the trout; but at present the only rivers which can be said to be inhabited by salmon, are those in Maine, Oregon, and California. The former are pretty effectually closed with dams and nets, and in the latter, fish culture is just beginning to be needed. Properly, salmon culture should be the heading of this article, or should take precedence of trout culture, but for these reasons the inferior fish is placed as the title, although we shall take up the management of the salmon first, as its treatment was first discovered, and its manipulation is the most complicated. Under the head of Salmon, may be included the salmon, the trout, the salmon-trout, otherwise called lake trout, the whitefish, the grayling, the fresh-water herring or cisco, and California brook trout, and the California salmon. The scientific names of these are, *salmo salar, salmo fontinalis, salmo confinis, salmo amethystus, coregonus albus, thymallus signifer, and salmo quinnat* These are all essentially alike in their mode of culture, the differences being so inconsiderable that they may be disregarded for the present. We shall speak of one for the whole, only occasionally pointing out such individualities as may be necessary.

They spawn in the autumn and winter, with the exception of the California salmon, which is earlier, and spawns in summer and first of autumn, the grayling, a fish of the same race, which has lately been found to exist in our country, and which spawns in March, and the California Brook trout which spawns in March and April.

The salmon comes in from the sea where he has passed the cold weather, as soon as the ice breaks up, and keeps on all summer long running up into the fresh water; which alone, is adapted to the fructification of his eggs. Trout in like manner, pass from the ponds and deep lakes into the cooler streams, where a constant supply of fresh and lively water can be obtained; whitefish appear from the depths of the great lakes and seeking the shallows along shore, select gravelly and rocky reefs and springy spots to lay their eggs.

Salmon and trout make nests, the females digging out the bottom and fanning away with their fins and tails the mud and finer sand from the gravel which they afterwards use to cover their eggs, and preparing a regular inchoate city of fish fry. When these operations are sufficiently advanced, the male who has been chosen by what Darwin curiously styles " natural selection," that is, a most bitter battle against all comers for the lady in "orange silk or silver lawn," who falls a prize to the strongest, joins his bride. They simultaneously and with one mutual impulse of amatory passion deposit the eggs of the female and milt of the male. Only a certain number of these are extruded at a single impulse, and are then carefully covered over with gravel by the female, while the male divides his time between driving away intruders of his own sex, who would usurp his prerogatives and devouring such stray eggs as may have escaped the notice of his devoted wife, and been carried down stream by the current. One noticeable peculiarity of the spawn of this class of fish is, that the moment it falls from the parent it adheres to whatever it touches. This is a provision of nature to enable the parent to cover it over with gravel before it is washed away, which she does with remarkable skill and care, moving the stones with her ventral fins and tail for that purpose. It remains fast for the space of thirty minutes or so, and then becomes loose and is swept away by the current, a dainty morsel for whatever bird or fish or insect that comes across it. It is also to be observed that the eggs are heavy and sink to the bottom like shot; a marked peculiarity of the spawn of the *salmonidae*, and distinguishing them from those of other varieties.

Several different deposits of spawn are made and covered up in this way till often quite a mound of fish eggs and gravel is erected. Such mounds built by the famous trout of Rangeley and her sister lakes are large enough to fill a two bushel basket. The operation of emitting the eggs is not all done at one time or on one day, it occupies several days, as will be more fully explained hereafter. As soon as the nest is completed, and the father and mother are exhausted of spawn and milt, they drop back worn out and weakly to the deeper water or the ocean, to recuperate. The eggs are left to themselves unprotected, except for their gravelly covering, and a prey to every passing spoiler. They were intended to be mainly destroyed, and that intention is effectually carried out.

A similar over supply or wastefulness of nature is visible in all its departments. Seeds of plants and trees are produced by millions to perish by millions, leaving only a few to fructify. Of these few even, but a small per centage lives and reaches maturity. Who has not noticed the innumerable seeds falling from the trees in early autumn, has not seen them driven about by the wind, swept into rows one on the other, carried into the water, crowded into holes and covered up by leaves. Next year out of the countless multitudes, some hundreds start into life, but they are by the way side or on stony ground, or amid weeds, or under the shade of stronger plants. The sun burns some, the shade kills others, the ground starves still more, the ranker growth destroys its share, and so they perish miserably, the exception being if a single one survives. We can partly guess why this superfluity exists, we can connect it in a measure with man's exactions and neccessities.

Enemies of fish life are numerous. First, and most to be dreaded in waters where they exist, are the eels. These are most difficult to exclude from the troughs and ponds. They devour eggs or young with equal voracity. Seven young trout have been taken from an eel six inches long and no thicker than a fine knitting needle; they grow as they eat, hiding most cunningly in the sand or gravel from human eye, and making their way through narrow passages and small holes that a person would not suspect them of being able to enter. One half grown eel will destroy an unlimited number of trout fry or eggs. Ducks are equally destructive, thrusting their long bills down into the nests of spawn, or seizing and swallowing the young; frogs, mice, rats, fish, many birds, and animals, and the larvae of beetles and devil's darning-needles, and other water flies before they have developed into the perfect insects do their share of damage. Most water creatures love fish spawn as most human creatures admire omelettes.

Unpromising as all this is, however, for a good crop of trout in the natural way, it is only the beginning of the trouble. The danger of disease or physical injury is always present. Heavy rains come and foul the water; when this settles the silt or sediment covers the whole batch of eggs, and smothers the life out of them. *Conferva* makes its appearance and soon spreads from one to another killing all it touches, and seems to be contagious, as a single dead egg will affect all those which are near it till the infection spreads through the entire heap. Accident or a great flood may even disturb the whole and leave the displaced eggs to perish miserably wherever they may be carried by the water. Amid such vicissitudes the wonder is not that so many perish but that any survive, and the need of nature's superfluity is thus made manifest. Exposed to all these dangers the eggs of the *salmonidæ* must remain in their natural defencelessness for from two to five months, according to the temperature of the water. A very large percentage fail to become impregnated, the current of water probably washing away the milt of the male before the sperms could enter the eggs. Mr. Livingston Stone says that in digging up some spawn of the California salmon, deposited by the parents in the natural manner, in the McCloud river, he found only eight per cent. vitalized.

When the little embryo of piscatory life has manfully braved these perils and has escaped from his shell, he is still by no means through his troubles. In the first place, his physical conformation is much against him; he is encumbered by a belly which would do credit to any alderman. In fact, the belly is the larger part of him, and, unlike that of his political prototype this impediment does not represent so many fat capons and good dinners which have been duly eaten and enjoyed, but represents a certain number of dinners for the future. For almost thirty days after birth the salmon or trout eats nothing but is sustained by the absorption of this stomach or what is more accurately termed the umbilical sac. All this while as may be readily understood, he is awkward and hampered in his movements, an easy prey to any hungry enemy. Appreciating his position he strives to hide himself during this period; he crawls into holes and under stones, and often hides so effectually that when he has been artificially hatched his anxious foster father the breeder, never discovers what has became of him unless his breeding troughs are well made and free from worm holes. But in this, his hour of weakness his enemies never desert him, they stand by him from first to last. At that stage of his development every miserable shiner, dace and minnow is his master, a very great despair by comparison with his feebleness. Cruelly is the superiority exercised, for mercy does not exist in the watery kingdom. The predaceous insects are also on the alert doubly gratified at his increased size, and epidemics attack him more severely than ever, and sweep away thousands.

These are the perils which surround our coming fish on his way to development. In the natural method they all have full scope and free exercise. Is it astonishing then that not more than one in a thousand ever reach a marketable size or attain the dignity of itself being a father or mother? Moreover, at this point man steps in to help along the ruinous process. He has no use for the minnows, nor the merciless insects, nor the many worthless varieties of creatures which play such havoc, but he takes the best the water affords. The magnificent salmon in all the silvery glories of the sea, amid whose caves of coral and pearl he has been gathering size and splendor; or the soft skinned trout, as delicate of color as the finest tints of the artist's brush, and as soft to the touch as the finest velvet; or the monster *salmo amethystus*, the Mackinaw salmon of Lake Superior; or the white fish, whose silvery scales shine like burnished silver. Man takes the best and so upsets the equipoise of nature, which up to that time had by its checks and balances kept all varieties of living creatures at an established relative proportion. For every salmon he eats there are ten thousand fewer eggs for the water bugs and the minnows who will make up the loss out of those which are left. These embodiments of evil must be fed and grow more diligent in the search for food, the scarcer it becomes, still man keeps on with net, and spear, and hook, making yearly larger drafts as the human race increases and extending his machinery as the prey diminishes; so the whole system of nature is disarranged. The edible fishes at first diminish, then, as the process goes on in geometrical ratio they decrease more rapidly, and the operation becomes accelerated at every step, till the stream or lake which once abounded with excellent fish is utterly and absolutely denuded and left sterile, bare and unproductive. The insects have devoured the last edible fish which man's greediness had failed to reach. This has happened with so many of the ponds and water courses of our country that it is safe to say, fully one-half of the lakes, rivers and streams throughout the older states, at least, yield nothing of food for man.

Such a result is no trivial injury to the community. The vast extent of these sketches of water are but little understood by the people at large. There are in the State of New York alone 647 lakes, with an area of 466.457 acres, besides countless smaller ponds, and miles of river and stream. Fully a quarter of a million of acres of the public patrimony are thus allowed to go to ruin and decay for the want of proper knowledge and a little care. It would have been easy to have protected them; it is a far more serious matter to restore their ancient productiveness.

The sea fisheries are scarcely better off. Professor Spencer F. Baird, of the Smithsonian Institution, was appointed, under a law of Congress, Commissioner to examine into the condition of the National fisheries and the cause of the diminution of their yield. The *fact* of "diminution" is the present point on which Professor Baird says, his observations having been made on the Coast of New England: "The evidence of the most deplorable decrease in the supply of fish is only too clear; and so greatly and rapidly has this occurred, that fishing stations which in 1860 produced thousands of fish, now furnish only hundreds, or at that ratio, giving a diminution of quite nine-tenths and often more."

Before leaving this branch of our subject, it is well to consider the geographical distribution of trout dependent as this is upon the character of the water in different sections of the country.

Trout are found in all rivers in which salmon can hatch their young, but as they are not necessarily migratory, they often dwell where salmon cannot. Trout require a temperature of water never exceeding 70°. At 68° they begin to suffer; at 70°, unless there is a strong and broken current to give life to the water, they die rapidly, and not one will survive a temperature of 75°. It is simply manifest then that the Southern and Western rivers are not generally inhabitable for trout or salmon. Trout may be found in the head waters of such as rise in the Alleghany range of mountains, but salmon can exist in none of them. So also with sluggish, muddy rivers of Ohio, Indiana, Illinois, Missouri, and the vast central region of our continent. Throughout the entire section between the Alleghanies and Lake Superior and the Northern Mississippi, except in Northern Michigan, no trout are found, and then again not till you come to the Rocky Mountains. Trout and salmon, except in the matter of migration, are similar in their habits. The eggs of either may be hatched in the same boxes, with the same water, in about the same time, and under the same treatment. This is being done to-day by the New York Commissioners of Fisheries at the State Hatching House at Caledonia. There are trout, *salmo fontinalis*, salmon *salmo salar*, and lake trout *salmo confinis*, all being hatched side by side in the same building, in identical troughs and with the same water.

When we speak of the temperature of a pond or river, allowance must be made for springs to which fish will have recourse, precisely as men perishing in a room for air, would put their mouths to a knot-hole to breathe. If there are springs enough, trout will live in waters the body of which reaches a higher temperature than seventy-five. So also, a strong rush of water as with a cataract or rapids, will enable them to endure greater heat than they could otherwise stand. Still it is not safe to subject any of the eastern salmon or trout family to a permanent temperature higher than 65°. Salmon trout suffer most and die the first, at least when they are confined in a limited space with a small flow of water.

The first point in fish culture is to obtain the spawning fish in proper condition, for if the eggs are not mature or ripe, as it is usually called, not only are they useless, but the effort to extract them will kill the parent. Fish breeders who make the cultivation of trout a business, and there are many in this country, keep on hand in suitable ponds a supply of large fish. These are taken from the rivers which they are ascending to spawn, and are kept over from year to year. Connected with the ponds in which they are confined, is a race way, or long narrow trough which has a gravelled bottom, is covered with boards to exclude intrusive eyes, and in every way is made as attractive a nesting spot to the fish as possible. Into this they will proceed of themselves when they are ready to perform their allotted act of reproduction, and the breeder awaiting his opportunity, places a net at the mouth of the race and frightening them in, selects such as are ready for manipulation.

When in a perfectly ripe condition, the eggs lie free in the ovaries in the abdomen, and may be extruded by a gentle pressure downward along the sides of the fish, They are caught in a basin and are vitalized by coming in contact with the milt from the males, for the fish male and female are stripped indiscriminately into one common receptacle. Formerly, the practice obtained of having this basin full of water, under the idea that such arrangement more nearly reproduced the natural conditions, but subsequent discoveries led to a change of this method. The ova are fertilized by the spermatozoa of the milt entering through the micropyle and taking up board and lodging within.

It was ascertained however, in practice, that these spermatozoa, little tadpoles as they appear to be under the microscope, were not fond of water, and although very active when first emitted, soon perished in the water. They retained their vitality much longer when dropped among the ova in a comparatively dry state, and this is the method universally pursued at present. The result of the change was very great; on the earlier plan not more than one egg in three or four was vitalized, whereas now, fully ninety eight per cent. are made capable of producing young as we have already mentioned, and as will be more fully explained hereafter when we come to special and particular directions for each part of the process.

The eggs mature in comparative safety. Some die, of course, others were never properly impregnated, but the percentage is small, not more than five or ten per cent. of the whole. In the natural method probably not one in five hundred, certainly not one in a hundred survives to mature and produce a perfect fish. By the artificial plan, and at the lowest calculation, fully ninety in every hundred are saved and developed. Here is the great gain in fish culture. It is in the primary stages that the advantage is secured. Say that afterwards the perils are alike and still see the enormous difference in its favor. Allow that young fish after their birth are in continued peril of their lives; that enemies still pursue and waylay, no matter how they are bred; suppose that one-half of all that are born perish before attaining a marketable condition. In one case that half has to be taken from a supply already decimated, in the other nearly the full number is to be drawn upon. Of ten thousand eggs deposited in the natural method, only twenty or thirty hatch, one-half of these would give us but ten or fifteen full grown salmon, whereas with the care of man nine thousand can be hatched, and if one-half perish we should have remaining four thousand five hundred, a difference so great as to be almost incredible, yet these results are obtained with reasonable certainty by trained fish culturists who understand their business.

CHAPTER III.

TROUT PONDS.

LOCATION.—It is very easy with good spring water to raise a *few* trout anywhere in temperate latitudes. But to raise a large number requires care in the selection of a location. Plenty of pure spring water is the first and most essential requisite. The spring, or one of the springs, if there are several, should have a fall of two or three feet, and a fall of five to ten feet of the whole volume of water is decidedly advantageous. If the supply of water is very large, it diminishes the necessity of a fall. The water from a spring remains (near its source) at nearly the same temperature during the whole year, and is the best for Trout raising. The water from a brook which does not rise higher than sixty five degrees in summer, may be used to supply ponds for adult Trout; but spring water is not absolutely necessary for hatching purposes. It is not a good plan to dam up a stream which varies in volume, and so make ponds. There should be enough level land by the side of such a stream to make ponds supplied by the stream; and it is best to have a stream much greater in volume than is necessary for the ponds, so that there will always be a good supply of water, and there will be no trouble with the surplus water after a freshet. A good knowledge of the whole system of Trout Culture is essential in choosing the very best location. It is desirable to have your ponds near your house, or have a man in charge living at the ponds. Of course your Trout may never be molested, but "an ounce of prevention is worth a pound of cure."

LAYING OUT PONDS.—The diagram represents a series of ponds, in all of which the same water is used. This plan is generally considered the best, for several reasons. It economizes the water and space, and is most convenient for changing the fish from one pond to another. It is not necessary that the ponds should be in a straight line. Where the location demands it they may be turned so as to lie in a direction nearly or quite parallel with one another. This is easily done by bending the raceways, and lengthening them if necessary, only a curved raceway is sometimes not so convenient as if it were straight. The sides of the ponds may be walled up with stones, laid without mortar, unless the soil is very sandy. Wood may be better for the sides and bottoms, but we are inclined to think is not worth its expense. If the sides of the ponds are laid up with mortar, let it dry thoroughly before letting the water in; then let the water run through it two or three weeks, or long enough to purify the pond before putting any fish in it. It is as well to test it by putting in only a few fish at first; if the pond is not thoroughly purified the fish in it will turn blind. Ponds should not be built where much surface drainage will run into them; if they are so exposed the surface water should be carried off by a ditch around them. The Second and Third Ponds should receive an additional supply of water. The reason for this will be given further on. A general idea of the form and size of ponds can be gathered from the diagram without further explanation. If the supply of water is small, it is best to have as much fall between the ponds as the nature of the ground will allow. This fall aerates the water and makes it as good as new.

SHAPE OF PONDS.—Where the supply of water is large it matters very little about the shape of the ponds. The best shape we believe to be the pear-shape, figured in the plate; such a shape combining an equable flow of water in all directions and the greatest amount of surface, with the least difference in the temperature of the water. If the nature of the ground demands other shapes, the ponds should be made long, narrow and deep, rather than broad and shallow. The depth of the pond is indicated in the plate, and will answer for any size of ponds. It is better for any one wishing to raise a large number of fish, to have several series of ponds, than to attempt raising a larger number by increasing the size of the ponds. Fish do not feed so well in large ponds, are not so easily taken care of, and eat each other more.

RACEWAYS.—The Second and Third ponds should have a long, narrow raceway where the water enters—about thirty or forty feet long, four feet wide and six inches deep. The sides of the raceway should be made of one and a half inch plank, one foot in width. This will answer for both natural and artificial impregnation. The raceway is required not only for the purpose of spawning, but as a resort for the fish at all seasons of the year.

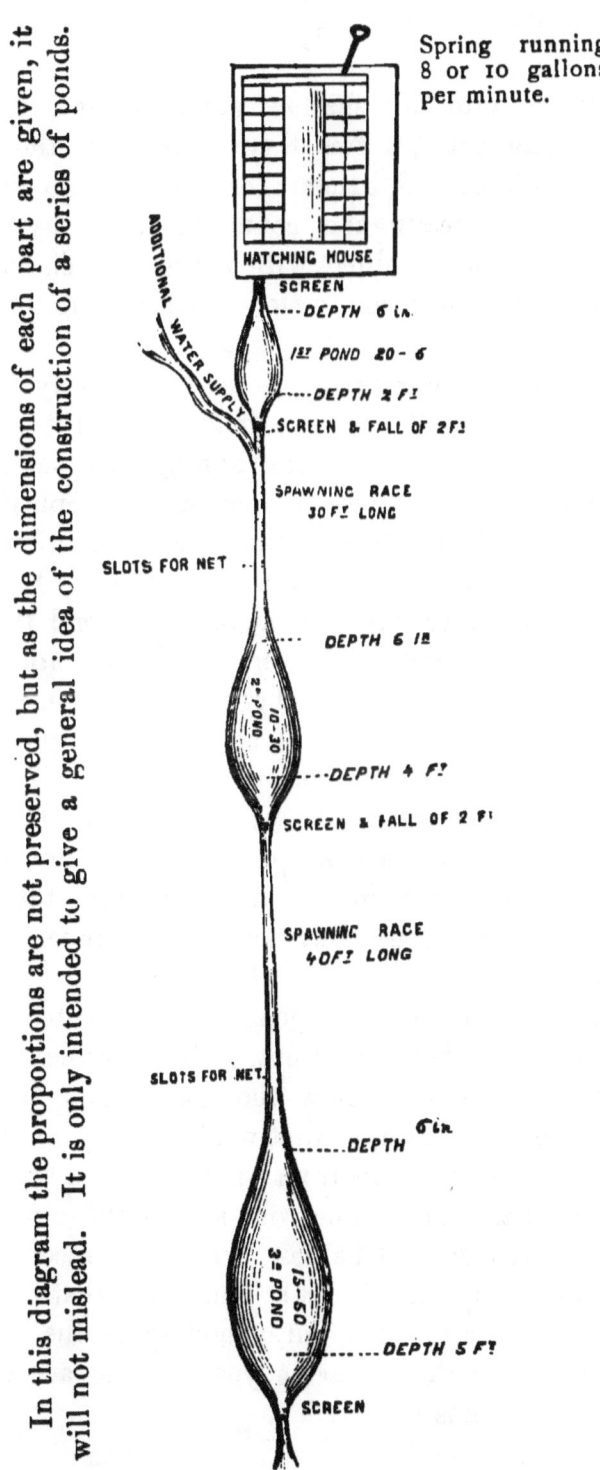

Fish will go into this shallow graveled race, into the quick running water, to free themselves from the parasites which often trouble them; or they will go there if they are out of health and condition from any cause. This raceway must be filled with coarse gravel, and the bottom of the pond made to slope gently up to the raceway.

The head of the raceway is to be carefully looked after. If a series of ponds are made, then the screens between will keep the fish from running from one to the other; but if single ponds are used, each supplied with separate water from a stream, then much attention must be paid to the screens where the water enters. It would be well if the water was brought into the pond through a long box, as the water will very soon work around or under a short box, and allow the fish to escape. If the water enters with a fall, it may be allowed to pour over upon an apron, constructed of thin slats, one-half or one-quarter of an inch apart, and set edgeways. This will let the water through and keep the fish from running up. Trout will run up stream very freely, working their way through a small passage, but will not try much to run down stream.

WILD RACEWAY.—If the ponds are connected with a stream in which there are trout, it is desirable if possible to make a raceway below the lowest dam and connect it with the stream, so that wild fish may use it. In this way a great many trout will be taken in a ripe condition that would otherwise spawn in some other part of the stream and be lost. The wild raceway has the advantage not merely of utilizing fish that have not cost any expense to keep, but of adding to the number of spawners for the following year by the addition of those that are thus captured.

BOTTOM OF PONDS.—It matters very little of what material the bottom is composed. Anything—mud, clay or moss is good, except gravel, and this is bad, not from the nature of the substance, but because the fish will spawn on it and the eggs be lost. Sometimes a person will wish to construct a pond in a place where there are springs, or to dam up the water and make a pond in a springy place. Under such circumstances it is a good plan to fill the bottom entirely with gravel, as the fish would spawn there in any case. For such a pond make the borders very shallow, so that the little fish may run up into the shallow water and escape from the large fish; or have the pond so arranged that after the fish have spawned they may be removed. Thus the eggs will hatch out and the little ones grow without danger. When the next season of spawning comes the little fish may be removed into another pond and the old ones let in again to spawn. Such a pond is good for any one wishing his establishment to run itself, as with a little care he can raise many fish in it without much trouble. But the gravel must not be smaller than a hickorynut, and from that to the size of a butternut.

Very often the bottom of a pond is porous and absorbs the water as fast as it runs in, so that there is hardly any running from the proper outlet. If you are short of water and wish to use all you can get for another pond, it is best to cement the bottom. If you have no further use for the water, it makes no difference how it goes off, that is if there are no holes in the bottom large enough to let the fish escape, and the water keeps up to its proper level. Weeds or mosses of any sort are not necessary at the bottom, and if the supply of water is not large they will speedily become a nuisance. The quantity of Trout food which they produce is of no account in an artificial pond where large numbers of Trout are kept, and they tend to foul the water by hiding dead fish and bits of meat. It is best, if possible, to have ponds so arranged that they can be entirely drained. This is necessary, sometimes, for cleaning or repairing them, and changing the fish from one pond to another. If the slope of the ground is sufficient to permit of such an arrangement, it will often save much labor in pumping or bailing. The drain pipe may be of pump logs, tile or pipe of any kind, and should be fixed in the lowest part of the bottom, or as near it as the level of the ground will allow. Still better would be a regular flume reaching from the bottom of the pond to the top. A bulkhead may be put in to raise the water as high as may be required, and a wire screen the whole size of the flume set a short distance in front of the bulkhead. This large screen has an additional advantage, as the larger the screen the less liable it is to clog up with leaves and moss, and the greater will be the volume of water passing through it.

SCREENS.—Screens may be made of common wire painted with tar—as will be described hereafter—of copper wire, or of galvanized iron wire. The last is the best, as it will last longest in proportion to its cost. The screens for keeping the small fry should be of fourteen threads to the inch, and for one year old fish five or six threads to the inch. Incline the screens at an angle of forty-five degrees, the top being farthest down stream. By inclining the screens in this manner a greater surface is exposed to the water than if they were placed perpendicularly. The sockets should be so made that the screens will fit tightly and yet be easily taken out to clean.

A very good screen for two and three year olds can be made from strips of lath planed and nailed to a strong frame, with quarter-inch openings between them. Or, what is better, the slats should be at least four inches wide so that if a leaf strikes against them it will catch without obstructing the flow of water and lie flat against a single slat, or if it reaches over the edge it will be carried through by the current striking upon one end. It cannot lap around the slat as it would if it were smaller. As for the width of the slats from one another the point to be guarded against is the fish running their heads through far enough to strike their eyes which will produce blindness. The distance they are to be apart will depend consequently, mainly on the size of the heads of the fish, and as fish grow at different rates of speed it will not do to go merely by their age, but for fair sized fish an opening of about five-eighths of an inch will answer. This refers to the upper screen, the lower screen, that at the foot of the pond, may be larger as the fish are more cautious about descending where they cannot see their way, just as a man will climb a hill in the dark at his best speed, but will go down very cautiously.

WATER SUPPLY.—It is immaterial what kind of water is used, whether hard or soft. Neither will so called "mineral water" hurt the trout unless the water is very stongly impregnated. Trout have been known to live and thrive in a stream one-sixth of whose volume was supplied by a strong sulphur spring. The essentials are that the stream shall be reasonably pure, the volume of water nearly uniform or so arranged that the supply taken from it is uniform and the temperature between thirty-six and sixty-five degrees.

One peculiar fact has been noticed in reference to the eggs which is important to those persons who collect eggs to impregnate and sell. The shells of those taken from trout living in limestone waters are found to be thicker and harder than those obtained from soft waters. This may come from the lime in the water, and is an advantage in rendering the eggs more easy to transport with safety, than where the shells are very delicate.

The supply of water necessary for a given number of trout is yet unsettled. For a series of ponds turning out one thousand large fish yearly, the water supply should fill a four inch pipe. This question will be treated more at length hereafter, but it is always safe to have as much water as possible, for within reasonable limits one can hardly have too much—that is to say, if the dams and sluices are solid, and the screens do not clog. It must not be forgotten that abundance of pure water is as essential to fish as abundance of pure air to man.

In saying that ponds must not have a gravelly bottom, we do not mean there should be no gravel. The trout must have access either to the raceway or some other spot of gravel to rub off parasites. This they cannot do if the bottom is wholly of mud and they are excluded from the raceway.

CHAPTER IV.

HATCHING HOUSE.

As a convenient illustration of a hatching house, we will present a view of the State establishment at Caledonia, as it was in the year 1875, the subsequent changes not being material to its efficiency. It is located on the stream where Mr. Seth Green had his original trout hatchery, and which is probably the finest site for the purpose in the United States. The source of Caledonia brook

NEW YORK STATE HATCHING HOUSE, AT CALEDONIA, N. Y.

is only about one mile above, and consists of immense springs which in some instances sprout from the ground, and in others form large ponds, and by their current drive mills. The stream is almost a river from its very start and is filled with subsidiary springs its entire course. An estimated flow of six barrels per second comes from some of the initial springs, and the temperature at the hatching house varies only 25°, from 35° to 60°, winter or summer. A record of the thermometer has been kept for years during the hatching season and is found to be restricted to a variation from November to March from 35° to 45°, and stands ordinarily about 36°; the springs themselves remaining invariably at 50°.

There is as little variation in the volume as in the temperature of the water, as the proximity to the source prevents the effect of freshets or drouths. The stream is simply one huge spring, and was for years famous for the vast number and excellent flavor of the trout it contained. It abounds with the natural food of trout, with insects, shrimp and larvae of water flies, and in the spring and even in winter the surface is covered with the *phryganidae* and *ephemeridae* as they issue forth in perfect form. The ground around the house is well adapted for constructing ponds, as there is at this spot a fall of four feet or thereabouts. The house itself is cheaply constructed of hemlock boards, and is fifty feet long by twenty feet wide, and is one and a half stories high. There is no attempt at ornament or elegance, and it is probably the plainest while the most efficient hatching house in the world. In it have been hatched in one season two million and a half of whitefish, two million salmon-trout, and one million and a half of brook trout together with several hundred thousand salmon, these figures not being taken by estimate but by actual count.

NEW YORK STATE HATCHING HOUSE—INTERIOR VIEW.

The accompanying plate and ground plan will readily show its arrangement, AA are troughs, forty feet long by fourteen inches wide and six inches deep inside measurement. These troughs are raised about one foot and a half above the floor for the sake of convenience in attending to the eggs. The supply pipe, D, sixty feet long and six inches deep, carries the water from the stream into the building, where it is received into the feed pipes, CC, in which filters are inserted before the faucets which admit the water into the troughs, AA. These troughs are used now especially for salmon and salmon trout eggs. OO are waste-pipes, by means of which any section of a trough can be cleaned without disturbing the rest. BB are the Holton hatching boxes.

The eggs are placed on trays made of wire cloth stretched on wooden frames. Each tray is twenty-seven inches long by fourteen inches wide, and will hold in a layer, one deep, 6,272 salmon trout eggs. Instead of using only one layer of these trays, it has been the practice for the last four years to use four layers in the upper sections and five in the lower sections; making for all the troughs a capacity of 534 trays, or, in round numbers, of three and one-half millions of salmon trout eggs.

With this illustration, we will proceed to give general direction for the construction and management of a hatching house.

SIZE AND MAKE.—If only a few eggs are to be hatched (say eight or ten thousand) no hatching house is necessary. The troughs may be placed in the open air, in any convenient place, and covered with a wire screen to keep out rats, mice and ducks. A light board cover must then be laid over them to shed the rain and snow and keep the eggs from exposure to the sunlight. A hatching house

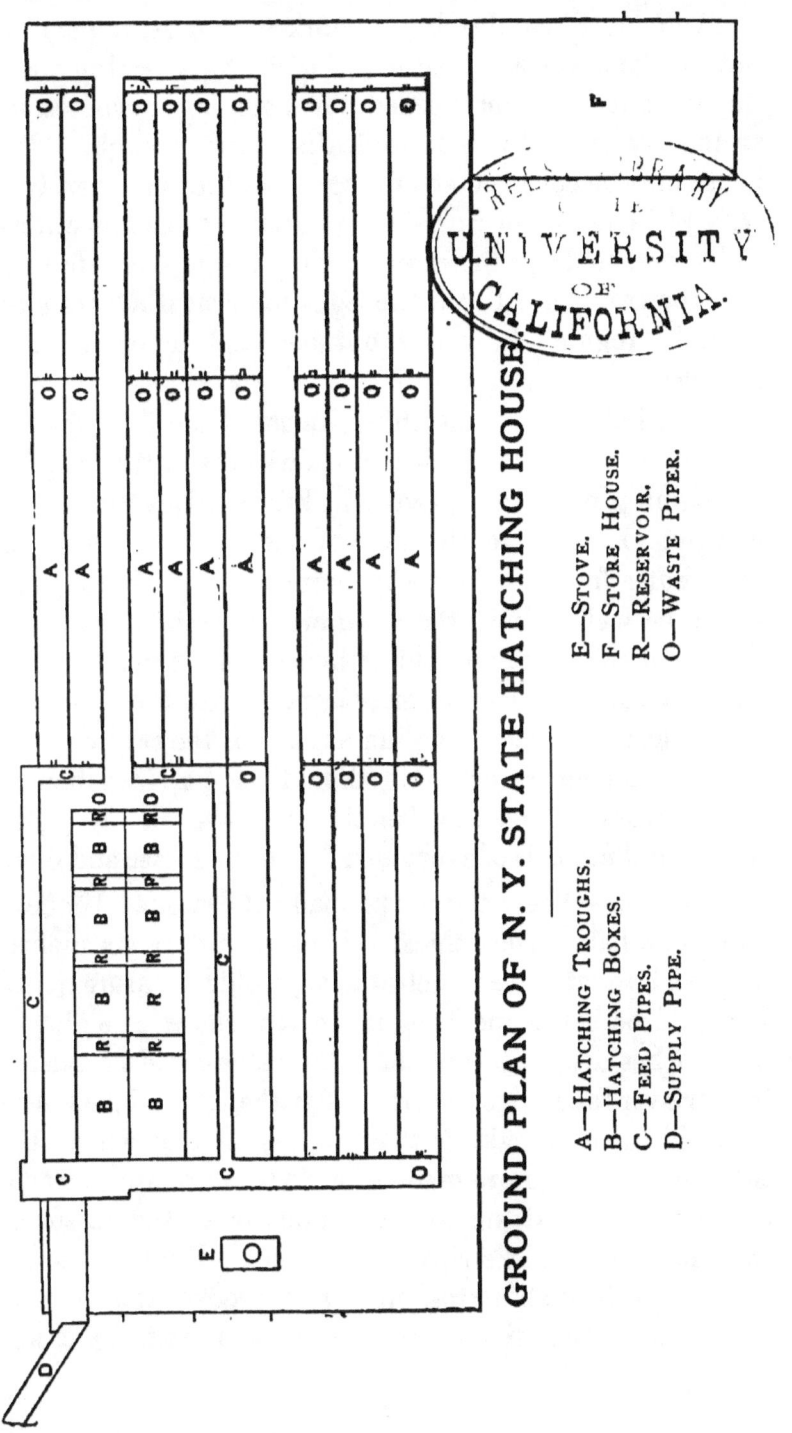

is much more comfortable to work in. A stove may be put in it and a fire started occasionally for warming one's fingers, but it is not needed for hatching purposes, as spring water in these latitudes is warm enough. The house may be constructed of rough boards, or as expensively as you choose, but care should be taken to have a water-tight roof, as drops of water leaking through and falling into the troughs will kill the eggs underneath. Its size must be regulated by the number and extent of the troughs.

The windows in a hatching house should be few in number and provided with curtains or shutters, as the sun shining upon the spawn will kill it. Not that a few minutes exposure to the rays of the sun will hurt the eggs, but a few hours exposure certainly will. Perhaps it would be well to have the windows, if possible, made on the north side of the hatching house, into which the sun will not shine in the winter season. Keep the hatching house clean. In fact cleanliness is one of the cardinal virtues to the trout raiser. He should have a clean house, should work with clean hands, and have all his pans, spoons and utensils of every sort free from grease and dirt.

TROUGHS.—These should be made of seasoned timber, one and a half inches thick. They should be six inches deep and about fifteen inches wide, inside measurement. It would be better, perhaps, if the troughs were eight or nine inches deep, because then the water could be raised higher over the the young trout after they are hatched out. The difficulty in making them so deep is that when the sides of the trough are made so wide they are apt to warp or stretch apart at the top, and must be stayed in some way; for instance, by strips nailed across. But the cleaner the trough is of all strips, elbows or grooves the better. The troughs are divided into squares or nests by cross strips set on the bottom at intervals of eighteen inches. The reason for this division into nests and for these cross strips will be seen further on. These strips may be made of half-inch stuff and cut two inches in width. There is no necessity for nailing them to the bottom; fit them in accurately and set them edgeways at intervals of eighteen inches. As they do not need to be removed often, it is better to make them fit tightly. Other strips of the same stuff must be provided, to fit upon these and made wide enough to raise the water within an inch of the top of the trough, as these need to be often moved they must be made loose enough to take out, and yet fit accurately enough to raise the water over them when they are put in. A groove is sometimes made in which to run the strips, or shoulders nailed to the sides against which to set them, but it interferes with the equable flow of the water. New wood under the action of water develops a slimy sap, therefore it is necessary to paint the troughs with hot coal tar mixed with enough turpentine to thin it to about the consistency of paint. Glass has been used to cover them, and the wood has been charred to prevent the growth of fungus, but nothing answers so well as gas tar, which should be used to cover every thing in the troughs or ponds, and where fungus can do harm. The troughs should have an inclination of about one inch in eight feet—just enough to let the wa'er ripple gently over the cross strips. They should not be longer than twenty feet, or the air in the water will be exhausted before the water reaches the end of the trough. There is more danger of this after the eggs are hatched out and the troughs are full of young fish. If possible the hatching house should be so far below the level of the spring from which its supply of water is derived, as to allow the troughs to be raised two or three feet from the floor. Where a large number of eggs are to be hatched, the inconvenience of stooping to care for them is very great.

WATER SUPPLY.—From the filter the water runs into the distributing trough or pipe, which runs along the head of all the hatching troughs. The water may be let into the hatching troughs by faucets, or through holes cut into the trough. These holes should be covered with netting, or the young fish will run up out of the troughs into the filter, or coarse gravel may be heaped up at the head of the trough through which the water will run, but through which the young fish cannot work their way. The supply of water for one trough should be equal to that coming through a three-fourth-inch hole with three inches head; just enough to make a gentle ripple over the cross-pieces. Be careful to get the troughs level crossways, and the strips true, so that when the water is running it will form an equal current over every part of each strip along the whole length of the trough. If the water runs unevenly the eggs will be washed into a heap if they are being hatched on gravel, and many of them spoiled for lack of proper circulation of water around them. This supply of water will be sufficient until the eggs are hatched out, when a somewhat larger supply can be allowed. The water should be brought directly from the spring in a pipe of some kind, in order to preserve the proper temperature and keep the water as free from sediment as possible; and for the same reason the spring should be walled up to its smallest possible dimensions. If any surface water naturally runs into the spring, a ditch should be dug around the spring to lead it off. If the muddy surface water is suffered to run into the spring which supplies the troughs, the screen will very soon be choked up, and the sediment will find its way into the troughs in spite of all precautions and destroy the eggs.

FILTER.—The filter is a box six feet long by one and a half feet wide and one and one-half feet deep; in which four or five flannel screens can be placed through which to filter the water before it passes into the troughs. The coarsest and cheapest red flannel is the best. It will rot and must be renewed once or twice in a season. Red flannel will last twice as long as any other. The flannel should be tacked on frames running in grooves set at an angle of forty-five degrees, (the top down stream) so as to expose as much surface as possible to the water. If the hatching house is small, the filter may be placed outside, but is better under cover. If the spring is well protected the screens will not need cleaning very frequently. They should be cleaned as soon as they look dirty, however often that may be, and can be cleaned best by being taken out and washed with a soft brush.

A filter can be made with sponges placed in a box with the water introduced at the top and brought out at the bottom, provided there is fall enough. The box should be about thirty inches long and twelve wide, and a board perforated with holes should be placed below the sponges, and leaving a space between them and the outlet pipe. This will answer on a moderate scale where only a small amount of water is used, and only a few hundred thousand fish hatched, and the sponges will remain clean for months. There should be an overflow pipe from the top to make sure that there is a sufficient supply of water and to carry off the surplus.

Sediment falling on the egg keeps the water off and destroys its life as effectually as being buried in the ground would destroy a man's life. If sediment falls upon the eggs it may be removed by gently agitating the eggs with a feather, or better still, by creating a current in the water with a feather, which current the eggs will follow, and as they roll over, the sediment will drop off. But the trout breeder has no business to be troubled in this way. If his apparatus is rightly constructed, and his filter properly attended to, there will not be sediment enough in the troughs to hurt the eggs, from the time they are put in until the fish are hatched out. The pipe which is let into the spring should have wire netting around it where the water comes in, to keep out impurities. This netting should be spread out so as to give a greater surface than the mouth of the pipe. If the netting covers only the mouth of the pipe, every speck of dirt which lodges on the netting diminishes by so much the supply of water; but if the surface of the netting is increased, much of it may be stopped up without lessening the supply of water. The best way is to make a box, say one foot square for each inch of diameter of the pipe, and run the pipe through a hole in the middle of the board, fitting it well; then fit a screen of netting on the front side in grooves so that it can be taken out and cleaned. This should be looked after occasionally, but if the spring is closely walled up, and the netting placed beneath the surface of the water, it will not probably need cleaning through the season.

GRAVEL FOR TROUGHS.—The gravel for the troughs should be quite fine—about the size of peas. It is better to use wire screens as will be explained hereafter, but where only a few eggs are to be hatched and it is important to avoid expensive preparations, gravel will answer. It was formerly used altogether but is now almost wholly discarded. It is better to have it of a uniform size. Any kind of gravel is good which is free from iron rust, as that kills the fish. If the gravel is of some dark tint, the dead eggs, which turn milk white, will show very plainly upon it, and may easily be picked out. The gravel should be well washed before use, and we would even recommend boiling it, to destroy any eggs of insects which may be adhering to it. After the nests are prepared the gravel may be put in, one and one-half inches deep, which will bring it within one-half inch of the top of the cross-piece.

IMPLEMENTS.—The implements of the fish-culturist are few and simple. A few feathers may be kept on hand to use in spreading the eggs when placing them in the troughs, in collecting them for packing, and moving them in the search after dead eggs. Several plans are in use for removing dead eggs from the trough. Some use a siphon to draw them up; others bend wire into the shape of a small spoon, or bend an eye upon the wire just large enough to hold the egg. We recommend the use of nippers. These may be made of wire or some elastic wood like red cedar, bent or cut into the shape of the letter U, elongated to about six inches, and with loops of wire at the ends about the eighth of an inch wide. These will hold the egg without trouble. A small homœpathic phial is used to examine the eggs. The manner of its use is to fill it with water, put in the eggs to be examined, cork it, hold it up before the window in a horizontal position, and with your microscope look *up* through the side of the phial. This brings the egg which lies at the bottom of the glass within the focus of the microscope, and the water does not distort its shape. This seems to be a very simple thing, and hardly worth telling but of the hundreds who have tried to examine eggs in our hatching house, not a half dozen got it right until told how to do it. The microscope need not be very strong; one magnifying eight or ten diameters is amply sufficient. A small net will be of use in removing the young fish and any refuse in the water from the troughs; it should be about 6 inches in diameter, in the shape of the letter D, with the handle on the middle of the bend. It is very easily made by bending a wire in the desired shape, and twisting the two ends together for a handle. Thin gauze of some kind, like bobinet should be spread over the wire so tightly that the middle of the net shall hang only a half inch below the level. An iron spoon, well tinned or silvered, is used to remove the eggs. Some six-quart tin milk-pans will be necessary, for a variety of purposes. Eggs may be counted most easily by measuring them. For this purpose take any small glass, such as a very small tumbler, for instance, count out 500 or a 1,000 eggs, and with a file make a mark upon the glass as high as they reach, and the measure is always ready to your hand.

A watering pot with a fine rose spout is used to wash sediment from the eggs on the scives, and a broom of wig s is used to brush the screens of wire.

CHAPTER V.

TREATMENT OF EGGS.

PLACING EGGS IN THE TROUGHS.—The eggs of a trout are about one-sixth of an inch in diameter, and nearly round. They are generally of a light straw or salmon color. The color varies with the meat of the fish. The redder the meat, the more orange colored are the eggs. They are generally of a light yellow or amber color at first, and grow darker as the egg grows older. Their specific gravity is a little greater than that of water, so that they will sink in water, but may be easily moved in it. Suppose the eggs to be obtained and that you have them in a shallow pan. The water in the troughs should be raised by placing a narrow strip across the trough upon one of the two inch strips dividing the nests. Then sink the pan gently to the edge in the water of the trough, at the same time tipping the pan, so that the water in the trough and in the pan shall come together with as little current as possible. Then the edge of the pan may be sunk into the water, and by tipping the pan a little more, the eggs will flow out without injury. By moving the pan while the eggs are running out, they may be spread uniformly over the bottom. If they fall in a heap, take the bearded end of a feather, and move the water with it in the direction you wish the eggs to go, and they will follow the current thus created. This may be done without touching the eggs with the feather. Distribute the eggs as evenly as possible over the surface of the nest. Where they are placed upon wire sieves, these may be moved and shaken under water so as to distribute the eggs evenly.

The strip which was placed across the trough to raise the water should then be removed. Care must be taken that it be not removed so suddenly as to cause a rush of water, which would carry most of the eggs away with it. Raise the strip a little way from the bottom so as to let the water run out gradually, and when it is very nearly or altogether at the proper level, the strip may be removed entirely. Those who have a nursery attached to the troughs place the earliest eggs in the lower end of the trough, and keep placing them toward the top, so that the fish which are first hatched can run first into the nursery without disturbing the others. We practice placing the eggs in the highest end of the trough first, because the eggs earliest placed, hatch out first, and the water should be raised over them, as they require more oxygen than the egg. If these first should be placed at the lower end of the trough, in order to do this the water must be raised over all the eggs; if at the upper end, strips can be placed upon the nests in succession as the eggs hatch out and the water left running upon the the unhatched eggs as usual. About ten thousand may be placed in each nest eighteen inches by fifteen inches.

If the eggs have been received from a trout breeder, they should be left in the packages in which they have been sent until the troughs are ready for them. Persons will sometimes take the tin boxes containing the eggs out of the saw dust in which they were packed, and set them in the water of their troughs, with the idea perhaps of getting the eggs in the box to the same temperature as the water before unpacking them. This will surely kill the eggs in a few hours. Leave them in the original package until a few hours before you are ready to place them in the troughs. Then take out the tins and set them over or near the troughs, which will reduce or raise the temperature enough. Then empty the box into a tin pan full of water taken from the trough, pick out as much moss as you can readily with your fingers or nippers, and wash off the nest in the manner shown in directions for washing eggs hereafter.

If the eggs have had decent treatment on the way, that is not thrown about roughly or set near a red hot stove, you should find very few dead eggs in the boxes, not more than ten or twelve in one thousand. Should the eggs be found, on opening the box, run together in lumps instead of being evenly distributed, and turned to a dead white or milky color, it shows rough usage on the way.

TEMPERATURE OF WATER AND TIME OF INCUBATION.—The length of time required to hatch out the eggs depends upon the temperature of the water. A general rule sufficiently accurate for all practical purposes is this: At fifty degrees trout eggs will hatch out in fifty days, each degree colder takes five days longer, and each degree warmer five days less. The difference however increasing as the temperature falls, and deminishing as it rises. The best temperature for hatching is between thirty-five and forty-five degrees. We are inclined to believe that the fish hatched at a temperature of about forty-five degrees and taking from seventy to seventy-five days to hatch, are stronger and longer lived, than those hatched in fifty days at fifty degrees. It may be well, also, to note that the eggs earliest taken produce the best fish. The water of a spring can be reduced in temperature in winter by letting it run for a short distance exposed to the open air, or it may be collected in a pond and the supply either drawn from the pond or the stream whichever is regarded as the most desirable. Another reason for delaying the hatching of trout is to bring them well into spring before they are turned loose, as at that time they can get more abundant food than they could earlier.

GROWTH IN THE EGG.—A great mistake is often made where eggs are to be distributed in retaining them too long after impregnation. This is sometimes done for convenience in shipping, and sometimes with a view of shortening the operation of hatching in the hands of the person receiving them, but it is all wrong.

About the twentieth day, the young fish can be plainly observed in the egg. Put a few eggs in a small phial and with a magnifying glass the formation of the fish can be easily seen. Fish farmers should send the eggs away at this time. Some of the eggs are not impregnated and at this stage of growth may easily be distinguished from the others. The dead eggs will turn to a milk or a pearl white color, and should be removed with the nippers as fast as they are discovered. If left in the trough a fungus growth forms upon them which extends to the other eggs in the immediate vicinity and kills them. Care should be taken in using nippers, not to hurt the other eggs, and to do this the bad egg should be feathered entirely separate from the rest; a very slight blow or jam from the nippers will be sufficient to destroy their vitality. Rats and mice in the hatching house often destroy many eggs; they are very fond of them, and going into the troughs to get them will destroy with their feet many more than they eat. A wire screen, or boards laid over the troughs will keep them out, but it is a much cheaper way and just as effectual, to keep them down by traps or poison. The eggs should be feathered over occasionally so that their whole surface may be exposed to the action of the water.

TRANSPORTATION OF EGGS.—Eggs should be packed in round tin boxes, about three inches wide and two and one-half inches deep; a few small holes are punched in the bottom to let the water run off, as water left in the box will kill the eggs. Specimens of eggs from different parts of the square are first examined with the microscope to see if a good percentage is impregnated. If they are, a six-quart pan is filled with water to the heighth of the box in which the eggs are to be packed. The bottom of the box is then covered with moss, and the box placed in the pan and filled with water. The moss used is that which grows in swamps, or on stones and timbers, in wet places, such as the stones in a brook, or the timbers of an old dam. It may be collected and kept all winter in a damp place in the hatching-house. The bottom of the tin is filled with a piece of this moss, somewhat depressed in the middle, so that the eggs shall not touch the sides of the box, the moss having previously been well washed to free it from dirt and insects. The moss to be used in packing must undergo a little more preparation. The green fibres must be cut with a pair of scissors from the roots. Only the green, soft and living fibres are used, and the roots, stems and dead leaves thrown away as useless. This fine moss must then be washed thoroughly. A very convenient way is to nail wire netting over the bottom of an old soap box. Cut the moss into this, and dipping it into water wash thoroughly so as to remove all dirt and insects, the latter being often injurous to the eggs. By simply lifting the box out of the water, you drain the moss.

The eggs are then taken out of the trough, by being brushed with a feather into a spoon. If you wish to count them, fill your glass measure with water, and turn the contents of the spoon into it. When the five hundred or thousand eggs are measured, pour them into a ladle (small enough to go inside of the packing box), having previously filled the ladle with water; then sink the ladle beneath the water in the packing box, and by gently tipping and shaking it the eggs will fall to the bottom of the box; where they may be spread evenly over the moss with a feather. A layer of prepared moss must then be lightly laid over the eggs without taking the box entirely out of the water, and another five hundred or thousand eggs put in. Then fill the box with the same kind of moss, take it out of the water and let it stand a little while so that the water may drain off through the holes in the bottom, and the damp, spongy moss be left, an elastic and life-giving cushion to keep the eggs from feeling sudden jolts on the journey, and to supply them with oxygen. It will drain more quickly if a chip is placed under the bottom at one side. When the water is all drained off the covers are to be placed on the boxes, and tied on with pack thread. If in any of these operations the box of eggs should fall out of your hands to the floor, it would probably kill nearly every egg.

The tin boxes are to be packed in saw dust in a box or pail, the saw dust being first very slightly dampened. The pail or box should have a handle so that the expressmen may lift it and set it down lightly, and not be tempted by the light weight of a square box to pitch it about and destroy every egg in it. The saw dust should cover the boxes to the depth of an inch, at least; then, if they are not exposed to a freezing temperature, nor to a hot fire, and receive moderately fair treatment, they will go safely thousands of miles. We have sent them beyond the Rocky Mountains, to California, to England, and to France. We have packed eggs in such a box when they were first taken from the fish, and keeping it at the same temperature as the water in the troughs, have left it until eggs taken at the same time and placed in the troughs, were hatching out; and then, opening the box, have found that some of the fish had already appeared, others were just breaking the shells, and all the impregnated eggs were alive, and in good condition. Of course the young fish did not live in the moss, but would die as soon as they appeared. We do not mention this as a new method of hatching eggs, but to show how perfect the means is of sending them.

The eggs in the box should be spread as thinly and evenly through the box as possible, taking care that none of them touch the sides, and the moss packed in well (not tightly) to keep them in place. If this is not done the recipient of the eggs will sometimes find them, after a long journey, jolted together into a solid mass, and spoiled. Use clean, bright tin boxes, which are free from iron rust, as rust on the tin or on the trays or screens which the eggs touch will kill them to a cetainty.

We have given this as the best method of shipping eggs, but larger boxes may be used for salmon eggs if large numbers are to be shipped and it is important to reduce labor to the minimum. In such case a partition of thin board should separate the box into two or more divisions and be supported by strips of wood so as to support the moss and eggs above. If these boxes are then packed in open crates in hay, straw or saw dust, ice may be placed above them and allowed to drip on the crates and among the straw, if they are to be exposed for a long time to hot weather.

They may be advantageously sent in refrigerator cars which are kept at a uniform temperature, or in the compartment of vessels appropriated to the shipment of fresh meat. The eggs of the California salmon have been safely sent to New Zealand. In 1876 shipments of eggs were made from San Francisco to New Zealand and arrived in such good order that over seventy-five per cent. of them hatched. The eggs after being packed, had to be carried two miles over a rough road, with the thermometer 104 degrees in the shade, then taken by railroad three hundred miles, and finally transported by steamer over seven thousand miles to the antipodes, crossing the equator on the way. So it is apparent there is little difficulty in transporting salmon eggs.

Another plan is to make a box of about a foot square with trays like drawers to slide into it and fit on one-another, which are kept in place by a door to the front of the box. The trays are nearly an inch deep, and are merely strips of wood nailed in the shape of a square with a bottom of canton flannel. The upper drawer has a lid of canton flannel also. The trays are placed in water, the eggs are spread carefully in them till they are full, and then they are put in the box. As the bottom of one rests on the top of the other the eggs are kept in place. Such a box will hold an immense number of eggs, but is only suited to being sent by a messenger who will take charge of it, and cannot be trusted to express.

CHAPTER VI.

YOUNG TROUT AND SALMON.

APPEARANCE.—After the eggs have lain in the water from fifty to seventy-five days, according to the temperature, the Trout will begin to make their appearance, the egg appears to be endowed with life, and the motions of the Trout inside "kicking" against the shell to force their way out can be plainly perceived without the use of a microscope. At length the Trout forces his way through, head first or tail first, those that hatch head first always dying however, and the useless shell floats away down stream. The Trout is then about one-half inch long, and the body proper as thin as a needle; the most prominent features being a pair of eyes, huge in comparison with the rest of the body, and a sac nearly as large as the egg. This sac is attached to the belly of the fish, and contains food, which the fish gradually absorbs. If the fish are hatched in fifty days the sac lasts about thirty, if in seventy days, about forty-five. At this period of their lives they will work down into the crevices of the gravel and along the sides of the troughs and stay there, nature seeming to give them the instinct at this weak and defenceless period of their lives, when they are burdened with a load which they can hardly carry, to get out of sight and out of the way of harm as much as possible. At this stage of their growth many curious deformities appear, more interesting perhaps to the physiologist than to Trout culturist. Some of the fry will have two heads, and some will be united after the manner of the Siamese Twins. A very common deformity is a crook or bend in the Trout, giving it a semi-circular form, so that when it attempts to swim it can only progress in small circles. All the deformed soon die, and may as well be removed from the trough at once. They live as long as the sac supplies them with food; when the sac is exhausted they cannot swim about to get food, and die of starvation.

This instinct of hiding will make the young fry very uneasy if they are placed in a trough without gravel. They will keep continually in motion, or will crowd upon one another in masses each trying to work his way out of sight under the others. They must now be watched, and carefully moved from time to time if there is danger of their smothering.

NURSERY.—The most critical period in the life of a Trout commences when the umbilical sac is absorbed. More, perhaps die from the time they begin to feed until they are six months old, than at any other time. In consequence many different plans for nurseries have been suggested and used. The fry require a largely increased supply of water, but where only a moderate number is to be raised, in place of erecting other and wider troughs or boxes for nurseries, the better plan is to put only a few eggs, say five hundred, into each square or nest of the hatching trough. The square is then large enough with the water raised to keep the Trout well for a month or two after they commence feeding, when they may be transferred into the first or upper pond. This plan economizes space, saves one removal, and the fish do better after a month or two in the ponds than they would in troughs or rearing boxes. It is better to remove the gravel from the troughs as soon as the fish commence feeding, because then the troughs can be kept clean more easily, else particles of food will lodge in the gravel, whence they cannot be removed. The water must be raised by the cross-strip before mentioned as soon as the eggs hatch out. It would be well to fix a small screen in each alternate cross-strip, which can be done by cutting out a space of eight inches by two, and nailing a fine screen over the opening. This will prevent the Trout from running up and down in the troughs, and inconveniently crowding together.

The fry are removed from the troughs into the pond by the use of a small net, such as described among the implements of the fish raiser. Take them upon this, a few at a time, and put them in a pan of water; they will swim off the net and you may draw it from under them. In the pan they may be carried, a thousand at a time, to the pond in which you wish to place them. Put them into still water; they will settle down on the bottom and remain there for some hours, then they will begin to explore their new quarters, and in a few days will become thoroughly habituated to the place.

Boards are sometimes placed over the outer edges of the preserves to give the fish a hiding place and shelter from the sun when they wish it, and more important than all, to act as a trap for minks in case there is danger of these destructive creatures getting into the ponds; as the boards project nine or ten inches from the sides, if a mink gets in he cannot make his way out.

Where a large number of fry are hatched they have to be left in the troughs until they can be distributed, which is done as soon after the absortion of the a possible. In this case the troughs must have all the gravel removed and must be kept scrupulously clean. A very little decayed meat will render the water offensive and produce disease. This offensiveness does not show itself in the least in the appearance of the water, which to the eye may be as bright, clean and sparkling as ever. It can, however, be often detected by the smell. When gravel has been for some time in the tanks or troughs where fish are fed—even with the utmost care, if a handfull is taken up it will be found to be very offensive to the olfactories. As well might we expect the human race to be healthy in foul atmosphere, as fish to be healthy in foul water. In the ponds it will sometimes answer to cover up or deoderise the feculent matter by throwing earth mixed with a very little salt into the water and allowing it to settle; this not only covers the decaying substances but disinfects them in a measure, on the principle that dry earth is used in the earth closet. The water is to be made quite thick and muddy with the earth, and the operation is to be renewed every few days, as often as necessary. The roiliness of the water does not seem to injure the fish. This, however, at best is but a makeshift, and the true plan, especially with young fry is to keep the troughs clean.

Cleaning the troughs must be peformed daily, in the morning and evening. A thin board nearly as wide as the trough and shaped like a hand shovel, is made with a short stick for a handle nailed across it. When this is held in the water across the trough it creates a strong current under it. It is held in the left hand while in the right hand is a small brush broom such as is used in cleaning sinks, and with which the sides and bottom of the trough are well scrubbed. All the dirt is sucked under the board and carried along to the lower end of the trough. The fish are also crowded together ahead of the cleaning operation and out of the way of the broom. When the lower part is reached the fry are driven above and the operation completed by netting out the larger pieces of meat or dirt, and by rubbing the finer particles through the screen at the lower end of the trough; or, a high cross bar may be put in, the screen raised for a moment and the waste plug opened.

When there is not accommodation in the troughs for all the fry and they can not be distributed, a temporary place of retention may be made by using the shad boxes which are described under the chapter on shad hatching. These need not generally be set at an angle to the current, as the mere ordinary disturbance of the water near the outlet of the ponds will give them motion enough to change the water. These will only answer temporarily and must be cleaned as carefully as the troughs. They are to be scrubbed all over the inside and on the bottom. To do this without injuring the fish, the box is tipped up so as to bring one part after the other out of the water where it can be brushed, while the fry are safely swimming at the other end.

If the fry must be kept in confinement, absolute cleanliness is a necessary prerequisite to their health; but we can not too strongly impress upon our readers the desirability of turning them out into the small rivulets connected with the waters where they are to live, as soon as possible after the sac is absorbed. Although they encounter some perils to which they are not exposed if kept in preserves, they escape still more dangers and acquire the habit of taking care of themselves which is necessary when they come finally to be thrown upon their own resources.

Food.—The best food for trout fry is raw liver, chopped as fine as possible, and then rubbed through a screen or sieve with a flat stick. It must be reduced to the consistency of pulp, and contain no strings or gristle. A chopping machine is made for chopping hash and sausage, and either that, or a couple of sharp knives are used to chop the liver. What is used is mixed with water so as to reduce it to about the thickness of cream. A teacup full of this mixture will feed a hundred thousand fish when they first begin to feed. The best way to feed them is to take a case-knife, dip it in the food and *slirt* off what adheres into the troughs; a very simple way, but one answering all practical purposes. Care should be taken not to feed too much, else the surplus food will remain on the bottom, and decaying there foul the trough. The reason of the difficulty in raising young fish appears to be that they are literally starved to death. The food which we can give them is not natural to them, it is often given in such coarse pieces that they cannot take it, and sometimes, through the carelessness of a hired hand, they are neglected two or three days at a time.

It is impossible to get the natural food for the fry, in fact no one knows what it is, further than that it must be microscopic insects of some sort, as the adult trout are never known to feed on anything but animal food. It is found in the spring runs, even actually in them, as they apparently issue bare of life from the bosom of the earth. Liver is but a poor and unnatural substitute for this food with fish so delicate as the trout, and if they once get the habit of feeding naturally on what the water offers they will not take the artificial food afterward. Fish, of any age, learn to eat that food which is most abundant around them. Anglers know this by experience, and use the flies which they see on the stream on which they are fish ing. It is supposed that a trout is very fond of grasshoppers, but the trout in one of our ponds which we have fed for a long time with beef lights, will not look at grasshoppers, and will turn up their noses at the fattest and juiciest worms, while the trout fresh caught out of the stream, which we have put in a pond by themselves to educate, will for weeks refuse the daintiest bits of lights and liver. Hunger will after a time drive them to change their food; but with the young ones we cannot wait for this, as they will die off before they learn. As the fish grow older and stronger more food must be given to them; when six months old, a bowl full of liver will answer for a thousand. While the fish are young, feed often; six or eight times a day for the first two or three months; three times a day will do after three months until they are a year old.

Young salmon, young salmon trout, California mountain trout, and above all young California salmon are larger, have stronger appetite, and will accept coarser food. For them, although at first the liver should be made as fine as for trout when they are a few weeks old, it will be hardly necessary to dilute it at all, and in the course of a few months they will not only take the larger pieces, often tearing them apart, but will scorn the finer portion. At one time sour milk was almost exclusively used for feeding young fish, but it has been given up. Other foods have been tried, but with no better success. The fish will not thrive on any of them as well as they do on liver, and do not thrive on that as well as if it were a natural food.

As they grow older, other things may be substituted or may be added to it as a change. They are fond of the roe of other fish, of the spawn of the horse-foot or king-crab; of fish itself, and when they are large enough to eat minnows, no better food can be given them. Liver is too expensive when it has to be used alone for grown fish, and beef lights are usually added to it or used in place of it in a measure. It is miserable food however, much of it passing through the stomachs of the trout and salmon wholly undigested and collecting in the bottom of the ponds. It injures the digestive organs and must be deleterious to the health of the fish. Its only recommendation is that it is cheap. Maggots are bred on spoilt meat, hung over the ponds, and as they fall off and drop into the water are readily devoured, and make excellent food. Or a piece of spoilt meat may be placed in a deep bottle like a preserving bottle, and the flies that will collect in immense numbers during summer may be caught and emptied into the water. This trap will take many times its bulk of flies by being kept set all the time and emptied when any one is passing it. Flies are probably the best food that can be given to trout.

One difficulty with all this family of fish which is accustomed to seize its prey while in motion, is that they will very rarely pick up food from the bottom. To obviate this, a plan of keeping the food in motion has been carried out on a small scale by utilizing an invention made at the New York state works for hatching the eggs, called the Holton hatching box, which will be described more fully hereafter. The idea of this was to introduce the water from below and carry it over the top. A funnel shaped tin or wooden vessel is made with the apex below, the water entering this creates a current that prevents the particles of food from descending, and keeps them in motion. Credit for this application of the invention is due to Mr. Winans of Baltimore, but it is at best but partially successful, as the food soon becomes so washed by the water that the fish will reject it, even if they have taken it into their mouths.

GROWTH.—There will be a great difference in the growth of the fish noticeable after the first few weeks of their existence. Some, of course, will be larger and more vigorous than others from their birth; but of those apparently of the same size and health when one month old, some at six months will be four times the size of others; this, too, when grown in the same pond and under the same circumstances. They will begin to eat each other when very young. A Trout only a few weeks old begins to show symptoms of fight, and will kill his weaker brethren when they get in his way by biting a piece out of their tails. In two or three months, when some of them get to be double the size of others, they will swallow the smaller ones. We have taken a Trout one inch long out of another only two inches long. It would seem to be advantageous, therefore, to sort them out every little while, and put the same size by themselves; but in practice this is very difficult, and the less a trout of any size is handled, the better; besides, if they are fed well they lose their disposition to eat each other. Therefore, the trout of each year may be left by themselves with very little probability of losing more by cannibalism than would be killed in sorting out and removing.

Salmon and salmon-trout do not require so much care as trout. Salmon, both the eastern and western, prefer to remain in the strong current of the stream, and not in the quiet eddies or dead water like trout. In this way they receive the element in a purer and better aerated condition. They grow more rapidly, and are sooner out of danger of infantile diseases. A curious fact has been observed in reference to California salmon, and probably the same rule applies to all fish. They will grow much more rapidly in warmer water than in the cold spring water in which they were hatched. Nor does the change produce any dimunition of health. Fry taken from the hatching troughs and placed in tanks with the water at sixty degrees, became, in the course of five months, five times as large as those that remained in the water of a temperature of about thirty-five degrees. They were exceedingly active, very few of them died; they ate voraciously, and their colors were very remarkably brilliant.

California mountain trout are also more vigorous in every way than the eastern trout; they are not so handsome, having no carmine specks, and much duller colors on their sides and bellies, but they are hardy, lived well in confinement, and grow rapidly. They take a fly readily and furnish excellent sport to the fisherman, while their flesh which like that of our trout is sometimes white and sometimes red is not to be surpassed as food. So strong are they that they are difficult to manipulate in extracting the spawn from them. They are hard to hold and will only give down their milt or spawn when they are ready. The person handling them must wait for his opportunity. The only California trout which were ever acclimatized in the eartern states up to this time (1878,) were hatched and grown in the New York establishment. They commenced spawning March 14, 1878, three years after they were imported in the egg. They yielded more eggs than the eastern trout in proportion to their size, and the eggs were slightly larger. They continued spawning until May 25th, and began to hatch in forty-five days. By the report of the Utah Commissioner of 1878, it is said that the western trout spawn in May, but as no spawners were taken by the Commissioner and no eggs obtained by him, he may have been too late, and the fish which he obtained instead of being all males, as he supposed, may have been spent fish.

PRECAUTION AGAINST ESCAPE.—There will always be a difficulty in so arranging ponds, screens, outlets and inlets as to keep the young fry in their proper pond. The water is very apt to work holes around the screens, or rather around the boxes containing the screens. The young fry will make their way through a wonderfully small hole, no matter how long the distance may be. They will also get through between the screen and the socket, unless these are very well fitted together, and wherever there is a crack into which they can get their large heads, they will put them in so tightly that they cannot extricate themselves, but will die. In short, wherever you can run the big blade of a jack-knife, there the young trout will go. In making a pond for them, it is best to beat the edges with a spade until they are perfectly smooth, or, better yet, to put a board around the edges to the depth of a foot.

CLEANING SCREENS.—If the screens are not kept well cleaned, two consequences follow. First, the water runs over the top of the screens instead of through them, and the young trout escape; and second, when the screens are taken out to be cleaned a rush of water follows their removal, carrying away with it numbers of trout into the next pond. Whenever you are going to clean the screens drive all the trout from their vicinity, then take the screens out and wash them with a stiff brush. They may be first raked off with a rake if they are made of slats, and then taken out and cleaned. They will require attention always once and sometimes twice a day.

DISEASES.—This part of fish-raising is least understood as yet. After the egg sac is absorbed and the fry begin to swim about, a sick one is very easily distinguished. The healthy trout swim in the current with their heads up tream, darting about here and there after minute particles of food. The diseased ones wander about listlessly, wiming round and round continually. They may also be known by the size of their heads, which appear much arger than their bodies. The head of a young trout is he largest portion of the fish, even when well, but when ick the fish appears to be all head.

Before the food sac is gone the trout is often afflicted with a swelling over the sac; a membrane forms there, wells out large and is filled with a watery substance. We call the disease the "dropsy," or "blue swelling." Sometimes the trout may be saved by making an incision in the swelling and letting out the water; but as with are only a few of them are affected in this way, it is better for the fish culturist to hatch more eggs than he expects to raise than to bother with a surgery he does not understand. In other words, hatch more than you want, and keep the strongest and best.

There is a small worm which is one of the greatest enemies which the young fry have. It spins a web in the water to catch the young fish, just as a spider does on land to catch flies. The web is as perfect as that of the spider and as much mechanical ingenuity is displayed in its construction. It is made as quickly and in the same way as a spider's, by fastening the thread at different points and going back and forth until the web is finished. The threads are not strong enough to hold the young trout after the unbilical sac is absorbed, but the web will stick to the fins and get wound around the head and gills and soon kills the fish. It is even more destructive to white fish, which are much smaller than trout when first hatched. The threads spun by this worm seem to be much finer than the common spider's web, and they are not visible in the water until the sediment collects upon them. They can then be seen very plainly. The webs can not be spun where there is much current and can be easily seen in still water by a close observer.

But after all the principal causes of the death of trout are, first and foremost, starvation, nine-tenths of all the young that die are literally starved. Secondly, rough handling; the least twisting or wringing of a fish with the hands will kill it. Thirdly, lack of sufficient water, and fourthly, the temperature of the water. These four difficulties, all of which are preventable will account for the death of most of the fish that die.

SALMON PONDS.—In order to hatch salmon it is necessary to have ponds where they can be retained till they are ripe after they appear in the spring, although as they are migratory, it is impossible to keep them throughout the year. The pond must be larger than for trout with a larger brook or race connected with it. Salmon will even seek the outlet to spawn. They may be captured in nets from the brook if there is no race, or a net may be attached across a salmon river and the fish ponded below it. They are manipulated precisely like trout, and the eggs hatched in the same way. The young, after they are turned loose, which must be done in the upper waters of the salmon rivers—as they live in the strong current, they will themselves seek the smaller tributaries—remain in fresh water for one or two years. The California salmon that were allowed to escape in Caledonia brook because there was no demand for them in the State of New York, remained there for one year, and until the second summer after the winter in which they were hatched, when they all disappeared never to return. They evidently started to go to the sea, but as they had to pass over the falls of the Genesee which are some ninety six feet in height, they may not have got there and they certainly never got back. They had attained a length of about six inches and were a beautiful fish, bright, lively, quick, and of fine game qualities, for their size. If they were retained in fresh water by proper screens, and if the supply from California were to be relied upon as permanent, they would be suitable for stocking private preserves and would furnish excellent sport. They will probably not attain their full size in confinement, not over a few pounds, and those that have been turned loose in the waters of our State and left to their own free wills have disappeared never to be seen again. They may come back and we hope they will, but as salmon were never indigenous to the Hudson river or any river South of it on the Atlantic coast, there is no certainty of their adapting themselves to their new quarters and furnishing us with breeding fish on our coast.

It is alleged that the salmon of California all die after breeding. This, if true, is most unusual and unnatural, and does not accord with their great abundance in the Columbia, the McCloud and the other rivers of the Pacific coast. A portion of them undoubtedly do so, as their journey from the sea is a long and exhausting one, but many others no doubt escape observation and lingering along, gradually recovering from the labors of parturition, straggle back at all seasons of the year to the ocean their home of health, food and recovery. It is hardly to be supposed that the operations of the United States Commission in collecting the eggs of the California salmon can be long continued. Either the McCloud river will be exhausted by the excessive drain upon it or the Commission will be satisfied with the results of the experiment. It was probably not intended to establish the operation as a permanent undertaking. Enough salmon have been sent to the Eastern States to fairly test the question, whether their streams are adapted to the residence of these fish, and if success ensues, the efforts of the Commission will be more than rewarded, while if failure shall occur there will be no reason for further drafts upon waters in which *salmo quinnat* has his natural home. It is, therefore, questionable whether private fish preserves can be supplied from this source either through national or individual enterprise.

There is diversity of opinion as to the time when salmon go to the sea, and the length of time they remain there before they return. Of European and Eastern salmon it has been supposed that about one-half go to the sea in the Fall one year and a half after they were hatched and the others a year later, but some fish culturists contend that they all remain for two years, and others say they all go the very year of their birth. We know that California salmon which were hatched in November remained through the Spring and Summer and until the Summer following, and then disappeared substantially together. We can not tell where they went nor what they did, for we did not go with them.

It is said the European salmon returns six months later, and in the spring following his descent when he weighed a few ounces, in the shape of a grilse or young male salmon just arriving at the age of puberty of as many pounds as he formerly weighed ounces. That he again goes to the sea in the fall and the following spring reappears as a full grown salmon of eight or ten pounds. The better opinion would seem however, to allow them rather more time to attain such ample dimensions, as an increase from ounces to pounds is almost too much for six months efforts, even of the most ravenous appetite. As with the shad, it is probable that the females develop ova a year later than the males possess milt.

Mr. Wilmot the able and experienced fish culturist of Canada, who has devoted much attention to the breeding of salmon and has made many valuable and instructive experiments, asserts that salmon need not visit the fresh water, but will mature their eggs if they are confined entirely to salt water. This discovery if sustained by fuller investigation, would save expense and facilitate operations, and in order not to do him injustice, we quote his language as used before the meeting of the Fish Cultural Association in 1878, without however, endorsing his views from our own knowledge.

"I should feel inclined to give you some experiments I was engaged in last year with regard to the new mode of retaining fish in salt water. The eggs matured equally well in salt water as in fresh. Of course it is well understood that for many years back, in fact for centuries, naturalists have held that there was a necessity for salmon to go to fresh water to mature their eggs. Last season I was under the impression that the eggs of the salmon would mature if kept in salt water as well as in fresh, and in order to illustrate that, I instructed one of my assistants to retain in the salt-water pond a few parent salmon, while I put the rest in fresh-water ponds; and he did so, and took the eggs from them at the same time. There was no perceptible difference noticed in the hatching of the eggs from those fish last year. That being sufficient for me to go upon, this season I retained fifty or sixty salmon in the salt-water pond. The eggs matured just as well as those of the fish in the fresh water. They were manipulated, and showed as much vitality and life as those in the fresh water. They were hatched in fresh water, but the fish were kept in the salt-water cove."

CHAPTER VII.

ADULT TROUT.

SUPPLY OF WATER FOR GIVEN NUMBER OF TROUT.—This has never been accurately determined, and we do not know that any general rule can be given applicable to all times and places. The quantity required for any given number depends very much upon the temperature of the water,—a certain supply in cold weather sustaining many more in good condition than the same supply in hot weather. It is the same with trout as with mankind. If many people are packed together in a close room, they will soon begin to suffer; but will not feel the bad effects so soon in cold weather as in warm. Now the water contains the air upon which the trout lives, and the amount requisite depends upon the amount of air which is in the water. A still and smoothly flowing stream, with little vegetation in it, contains the least amount of air. Hence the value of a fall of water between the ponds if the stream is small. The volume of water required depends also upon the shape of the ponds and upon the size of the fish. We can only say *about* what quantity is necessary and leave each owner of ponds to observe for himself whether more or less fish do well with it.

It must always be borne in mind that the larger the supply of water the better for the trout; and the trout-breeder on a large scale will find better success with small ponds and large supply than in any other way. For ten thousand fish the stream should not be less than seven inches square (that is, forty-nine square inches) and would be still better if it was seventy-five square inches. A less supply will perhaps do; but with it there is danger of disease and death to the fish. We will say then a supply of water filling a pipe five inches square (making twenty-five square inches) for the size of ponds shown in plate on a previous page calculated to sustain five thousand fish in the second, and two thousand fish in the third ponds. The first pond to receive six or eight thousand young fish, need not have more than two or three square inches of the water. This estimate of number of fish is purposely made low. More fish *may* be able to live with the supply mentioned; but the number given *certainly* can.

GROWTH OF TROUT.—It is impossible to tell the age of a trout by its size, as its size depends very much upon the quantity of food which it obtains. It is a general rule that with good feeding a trout three years old will weigh one pound. They have been known to live for years at the bottom of a well, where the supply of food must have been extremely limited, and remain through all those years, apparently at the same size. Then again, with good feeding, they will more than double their weight in a single season. Trout will not grow so fast in swift running water as in a pond The largest trout are never caught in narrow parts of the stream where the water runs fast. But where the stream swells out into a dark and still pool, there the patriarchs are found. We presume that the largest trout now taken in this country are found in the lakes of Maine. Some will grow much faster than others under any circumstances. A few will always look lean and hungry no matter how much they are fed, and others seem to have a peculiar knack of getting fat. Still the rule of good feeding applies equally to all. They will not grow so fast when three or four years old as before; that is, the rate of increase diminishes with age. The average age of trout is perhaps twelve or fourteen years. On this point we cannot speak with certainty. We have seen trout grown from the egg and kept in confinement and well fed on beef lights and hearts that weighed in the spring after the year they were born, or say when not over fifteen months old, as much as three quarters of a pound in some instances, and all averaging a half pound apiece. Judging from those in our possession, we suppose a trout to be in its prime when it is from three to ten years old. The size is largely a question of food. On Long Island where they have access to the salt water and feed on the numberless small fish and crustacea abounding in the sea, the trout are notoriously large, while in the mountain streams, where the food is scarce and precarious, it is just as well known that the trout are small.

The size to which a trout may grow is not very well settled; so many "fish stories" have been told that discredit is thrown even upon well authenticated assertions. Trout may in exceptional cases and in large waters attain the weight of eight or ten pounds, but a four pound trout is generally considered to be of pretty good size. This question of size is interesting rather to the sportsman that to the trout farmer. It is considered that small trout are the best to eat, those from one-quarter to one-half a pound. A better market may always be found for fish of this size than for any other. There is only one market in the United States where there is a demand for very large trout, and that is New York, where the largest trout sell the most readily. Besides, fish of small size are the handiest to manage on the spawning bed, and more of them can be raised. If the spawn is extracted by hand, the difficulty in handling a two pound trout is very great and increases very fast as the fish grows larger. Not only is it troublesome to handle the large ones, but the danger of killing them is much greater; so that, in our opinion, from one-quarter to one pound weight is as large as the fish farmer should attempt to grow his trout, unless from motives of curiosity to see how large they will get to be.

As to the growth of salmon, we can say that in confinement in small stew ponds the California salmon will attain about the weight of three-quarters of a pound, and the Kennebec or Eastern salmon a little more. None of the California salmon had, when this was written, produced eggs while retained in the fresh water, but the milt is developed and has been used for fecundating trout and salmon trout eggs. When at liberty and allowed to visit the ocean, salmon grow much faster, and we take the following extract from the report of Maine Commissioners of Fisheries:

"SALMON. In our issue of May 3d, we made mention of a very large salmon caught at Cape Jellison, Stockton, by Josiah Parsons, and purchased by Frank Collins, of this city. The fish measured fifty inches in length and weighed thirty-three and a half pounds. Attached to the fish was a metallic tag numbered "1019," indicating that it was one liberated from the Bucksport Breeding Works. The tag was forwarded to Mr. Atkins, the superintendent of the works, who keeps a record of all fish used for spawing purposes and liberated. We now chronicle the record of the fish, as learned from a letter from Mr. Atkins to Mr. Collins. He writes that the salmon was liberated at Bucksport, Nov. 10, 1875. It was a female fish, thirty-nine and a half inches in length and yielded five pounds and six ounces of spawn, or about 16,000 eggs. After spawning, it weighed sixteen pounds. He judges that in the preceding May, (1875) the fish weighed twenty-five pounds. Thus the fish in two years had grown nearly an additional foot in length and eight and a half pounds in weight. One important fact in the habits of the salmon has been demonstrated by the use of these tags, and that is, that the fish, after it becomes large, does not visit the river every year, as was formerly supposed, but only every second year. Those liberated in the Penobscot in 1873, were recaptured in 1875, and those let loose in 1875 are now being caught. One dollar premium is paid for every tag thus found. The Penobscot river about Bangor is reported to be full of young salmon."

But it is very probable that both California and Penobscot salmon will spawn in fresh water if they have fair range, that is to say, a pond of good size. In Iowa, see Report of '75-7, p. 12, the Eastern salmon when in a pond, were said to have grown in two years and a half to weigh from two and a half to seven pounds; if this is so, and these were not salmon trout, there is no reason the California salmon should not grow as large, or nearly so.

COLOR.—A trout is always the color of the bottom over which it lies; and in passing from one color of bottom to another, it will change in a minute. The trout in deep and shaded pools are notoriously deeper in color, or rather darker than those in shallow, bright waters; and they not only look darker while they are in the water, but stay darker when they are removed. The trout-raiser must make his ponds accordingly: shallow and exposed if he wishes light-colored trout; deep and shaded if he wishes a darker color. Fish often become blind from various reasons in the ponds, and when they do so they turn very dark—black, one would almost say by comparison with the others. The cause of this is not clearly understood, and it would suggest that the fish have control over their own color and adapt it to what are their surroundings or are supposed by them to be. The trout becoming blind imagines that everything about him is black and so assimilates his own hue to it as nearly as he can. It is possible that the power is bestowed upon these creatures as a defence against predacious birds which can not see them so readily if they are the color of the bottom on which they are lying.

Food.—In keeping large numbers of fish either for breeding or for sale, the first thing to be determined is, what is the best food which can be obtained cheapest and in the greatest quantities. This question is important because the profit depends upon it. All other circumstances being equal, he who can obtain the cheapest food will make fish raising pay the best. In France and Germany dead animals are gathered from the farms around the fish establishments and made into *pates*, or pies, which are fed to the fish as wanted. However good this may be for the fish it is somewhat repugnant to the taste of the fish eater. In this country we pursue a cleaner method. The pluck of animals killed (that is the lights, liver and heart) is obtained from the butchers. This food can be obtained fresh at least once or twice a week in most localities and kept fresh by means of an ice house. In fact trout will not eat decayed or spoiled meat unless they are very hungry. They are very dainty in their tastes and will often go hungry rather than take anything which they do not fancy. We feed meat to them raw.

The lights should be given to the larger fish as it can not be chopped as fine as the liver and is more apt to hang in strips or strings. The liver which can easily be cut into small pieces may be fed to the smaller fish. Trout will sometimes choke to death; they are so greedy that they attempt to swallow a very large piece of food and it sticks in their throats and kills them. Often it it is caught in their teeth and thus prevented from going down the throat, or it gets into their gills and stops their breathing. They will, when choking, come to the top of the water, and may sometimes be saved by taking the piece out of their throats, or pushing it down. But the best remedy is to chop the meat fine, say one-half or one-quarter inch squares for two and three years old.

No machine which we have ever tried would do the work of chopping to our satisfaction. A sausage machine runs the food together and mashes it, and the meat cutters, which do the best, require cleaning and sharpening so often that they are only a nuisance. The best thing we have ever found is a butcher's block, or log of wood two and a half feet high on which to cut, and a very heavy knife or light butcher's cleaver. These instruments are very simple, not liable to get out of order, and do the work required of them in the best manner, and with no more labor than a machine would require. Sometimes two or three knives are fastened together to make the work go more expeditiously; but one is best, or at most one in each hand.

Fish fed on liver or lights are not as good eating as wild fish; this is especially so of trout, which should never be sent to market or the table directly from the stew pond. But they soon recover their flavor when they are turned loose, and made to seek their natural food in a natural way.

Any kind of meat is good for food. Trout are carnivorous and will not eat vegetables of any kind that we have ever tried. We feed them lights and liver because it is the least expensive food we can find in large quantities, and answers a very good purpose. In their natural state trout feed upon insects of all descriptions which abound in or near the water; worms of all sorts, from the angle worm to the caterpillar, which the wind shakes from the trees bordering the stream into the water, are eagerly taken. Flies of every kind which either drop down upon the surface of the water to lay their eggs, or may happen to fall into it, are quickly devoured. Young fish which may be in the stream serve for food; so do the grasshoppers and beetles which fall into the water, and even the crawfish is not spared. If any one will examine the bottom of a good trout stream carefully, he will find every stick, stone and bunch of moss in it covered and filled with insects of various kinds. If you look at the bottom of the creek, also, when it is free from moss and sticks, you will see that in the summer time it presents a curious mottled appearance, as if it were having an eruption of some kind; these protuberances are caused by the larvæ of water flies, which, after a time, rise to the surface, and then breaking their shell or case, for the first time, spread their wings and fly away. On these before they have assumed the fly-state, the trout feed; and the eggs of water flies, together with minute insects and worms are the special food of the very young trout.

Fish of any kind are a very good food for trout. If they are small they may be put into the water whole, the trout will take them all the better if they are alive. Any coarse fish which can be obtained cheaply and in sufficient quantities may be chopped up fine and used as food. As we said before, they will not eat carrion unless pressed by hunger. They will eat a live trout, but we have never known an instance of their eating, or even touching a dead one. If any way could be devised of raising flies, or shrimp, or various kinds of insects (their natural food) in sufficient quantities and at little expense, this would be the best of all. A change of food would also do them good, but we find that they will not readily change their food.

As to the quantity of food necessary for a given number of trout. This is difficult to give exactly as it will vary with the size of the fish and the season of the year, more being required in moderate weather than when it is very hot or very cold. For one thousand three year olds, about five pounds of light or liver per day; for two year olds three pounds; but a very little trial will show just how much to feed them. Feeding once each day will keep the trout, over one year old in good condition. Feed slowly, and as soon as they begin to refuse the food stop feeding them, then you have the measure and feed a little less than this quantity every day. We say a little less because we have known cases in which owners of ponds being over anxious to fatten their trout, have killed them by over-feeding. Still this does not often happen, especially if they are fed regularly. A trout after long abstinence will gorge himself to repletion; but will not kill himself to-day if he is reasonably sure of to-morrow's dinner. All animals appear to be wiser than men in this matter, and it is very seldom that they will eat enough to do them injury no matter how much may be given them.

Salmon and salmon trout as we have heretofore remarked will, when they are young accept food that is rather less finely prepared. Their food is of the same general kind, but as they are larger fish they need more of it. Salmon trout can be kept in confinement until they weigh ten or more pounds, whereas the largest tame trout we have had did not exceed four, but few reached three, it being doubtful whether fish ever attain as full development in the domesticated as in the wild state.

As salmon trout will grow to weigh a hundred pounds in Lake Superior, it is probable they may reach twenty in suitable preserves, although the largest we have is not over nine, but he is healthy and is still growing. Salmon trout have been taught to eat trout that died of a natural death, although they at first utterly refused such food they came in the end to accept it willingly. Trout seven inches long have been disposed of in that way.

Trout and salmon, the latter especially, will get so tame after a time that they will take the food out of your fingers, in fact they will take the fingers too. Their teeth are sharp and make scratches like needles. They may be taught to jump for their food by holding it a short distance above the water, or may be made to come up and take it out of the pan you are holding. Feed in the middle of the day when the sun is well up, any time from ten to three is good. Make it a general rule to feed slowly and give them as much as they will eat without wasting.

Although trout and salmon become so tame that they may be made pets, some hybrids in the state hatching works are so shy that they keep as much as possible out of sight, and can hardly be fed. They were a cross of the milt of the salmon with the brook trout eggs, and perhaps knew that they were monstrosities. There is a board covering to the edges of the preserve in which they are kept, and they hide under it and run hither and thither in fright and confusion if any one attempts to get a close view of them.

Salted food has been tried for the feeding of trout, but not with satisfactory results. They do not seem to like it although it is possible they might be accustomed to it if any important advantage was connected with its use. It, however, ordinarily costs as much or more than the fresh meats, and cannot be superior to them. There is much of the offal of large cities which may yet be utilized as fish food. Where it is allowed to go to waste and run into the rivers adjacent to markets, it invariably attracts wild fish to such places, and if it is satisfactory food for them, it would be equally agreeable to their tame and less particular brethren. The fish breeder must not rely upon getting his food of any kind for nothing, as although most country butchers throw away their beef lights, they will put a price on them the moment they find they are in demand. Three cents a pound is the price usually asked for such food, and at that it is doubtful whether trout can be bred and raised for the market even when they can be sold for a dollar a pound.

TEMPERATURE OF WATER.—The colder the water is, down to forty degrees, the better the trout will do. They will die in the ponds if the water rises to seventy degrees, unless there is a spring in the pond, or colder water into which they can get. We have often heard or seen the statement that fish could be kept in a frozen state a long while, and then thawed out and be as lively as ever. Our experience is against this. Fish may be frozen, so that a thin coat of ice forms over them, and so long as they can be bent they will thaw out and will recover; but if they are once frozen solid or stiff throughout, they are dead, and cannot be brought back to life. If the ponds freeze over in winter, it is no sign that the water under the ice is below thirty-two degrees. If it was, the water in the ponds would freeze solid. Unless the water is taken close to a spring and much water runs through the ponds, the surface *will* freeze over; but this will not injure the fish, as the water below will be much warmer than the temperature of the atmosphere; and the ice which forms over the pond serves to keep the water below from being made colder by contact with the air.

If the water is so sluggish as to be likely to rise above seventy degrees in summer, the ponds may be shaded in some way. Trees and bushes look very nicely about the borders of the ponds, and are very valuable so far as ornament is concerned. But there are certain objections to their use which will banish them pretty thoroughly from the grounds of the practical trout-raiser. One objection is that the leaves, in autumn especially, clog up the screens, and demand constant attention to prevent an overflow of the water and trout. Or the leaves fall to the bottom and decaying there, foul the pond. The roots of the trees also will force their way towards the water, and break the walls or banks of the pond. If it is necessary to shade the ponds, floats may be used, made of boards nailed together and moored in some convenient place; but the best plan of shading is by light covers placed on beams running across the pond. If the ponds are very large the floats will have to be used. But the ponds must not be made large. We have said that trout would not live in water which was raised above the temperature of seventy degrees, and would do better in water at forty degrees. This settles the question as to how far south trout will live in the ordinary rivers.

California salmon will stand a much higher temperature than trout. The McCloud river from which the eggs were obtained that have been distributed by the United States Fish Commissioner through the eastern states, often rises to 80 degrees, and occasionally as high as 83 degrees. Its temperature through a large part of the year is over 70 degrees, both at the surface and at the bottom, and yet the salmon did not seem to be injured by it. We have kept young California salmon in a preserve when the water rose above 80 degrees in temperature, and although the inlet was open and they could have gone out, as many of them did, others remained until we thought it better to drive them out by drawing off the water. However this temperature is not safe for them unless there is a large body of water or considerable motion to it which gives it life and enables the fish to live in it longer. In an aquarium in which there were pairs of Kennebec and California salmon, brook-trout, salmon-trout and grayling, when the water rose to 74 degrees they were greatly distressed, coming to the surface and gasping. When it reached 75 degrees they all died.

It must not be forgotten that in ponds there is often a spring to which the fish can have recourse and which will save their lives. It is not always possible to judge by the temperature of the surface, for that below may be lower, but it is better to be on the safe side as far as possible. The larger the fish the more they will suffer and the sooner they will die. They exhaust the oxygen much more rapidly than the fry.

Brook trout are only suitable for clear, cold water, of which the temperature never goes above 70°. Salmon trout will live only in clear, cold, deep lakes. They need the purest water of any fish in this country. In the aquarium above referred to were put brook trout, salmon trout, greyling, California and Kennebec salmon and California brook trout, and as the water became warm the salmon trout began to suffer first, and died before the mercury went up to 74°. The brook trout went next, the greyling next, the California brook trout fourth, the Kennebec salmon fifth, and the California salmon last.

The salmon trout died twelve hours before any of the rest, and all of the others died within four hours of each other. All of the full spawning fish want clear, cold water. Whitefish will not live in water above 72° We have seen these taken in a seine, and when they got into shallow water where the temperature was 74° ten rods from the shore, the fish began to "turn up," and were all dead when they were hauled up on the shore.

DISEASES AND ENEMIES.—The diseases to which adult trout are subject are numerous and often fatal. Sometimes a trout will be observed to have a white fungus growing upon it in spots. This will spread over the fish until it dies. Sometimes fish will turn to a black color. This always seems to be an indication of blindness, as we have never observed this peculiar color unless the fish was partially or totally blind. The fungus which grows upon the fish is probably not a disease, but is caused by, or is the indication of a disease. Nothing is known about remedies. If only a few trout are affected, take them out as they will be sure to die. If the trout begin to die in numbers, change them to another pond, if possible, or give them more water. This is all we can do for them. The dead trout should be taken out of the pond as fast as they are discovered. They will rise to the surface only in very rare cases, but generally sink to the bottom, and if there is much moss in the pond they are lost to sight, and decaying on the bottom will foul the pond. If there is much sickness among the trout, we generally consider it a sign of insufficient water.

There are but few enemies of trout in artificial ponds. If the ponds are near the house, and people constantly about them, there will be no trouble with the birds which usually prey upon fish—such as the kingfisher, fish-hawk and crane. Even if the ponds are some distance from the house, the water will probably be too deep for the fish-hawk and kingfisher to do much mischief, as it is only in shallow water that they can be certain of their prey. Cranes will wade into the water and take all that comes within reach of their long bills—whether frogs, snakes or fish. But they are very few in number, and the trout are wary. If any of these birds appear, shoot them. Muskrats sometimes get into the ponds. They can not often catch the trout, but will destroy the young and the spawn if they can get at the troughs, and they eat many of the insects on which the trout feed, besides they makes holes in the banks of the ponds and let the water off. A few traps will soon dispose of them. It may be worth while to mention here the manner of catching them. Find out the places where the muskrats go into the ponds. They will make a little bare path, or run on the edge of the bank, by always going in and out at the same place. Then set a trap (a common game trap, such as is sold in all country stores) in the water, so that the plate of the trap will come in the middle of the run and about a half an inch under water, taking care to place the jaws of the trap in such a direction that when shut they will be in a line with the run. Then stake the chain into deep water. No bait is necessary. If any bait is used a sweet apple or parsnip may be stuck on a stick and the stick stuck into the bank so as to bring the apple just over the jaws of the trap when closed. The muskrat comes through his run, steps on the pan of the trap and springs it. He tries to take it with him to the shore. If he succeeds in doing this, he will likely get out in some way; for instance, if he is caught by the leg, he will sit down and knaw it off, in order to get free. But as the trap is staked out into the water, he can not get to shore, and will be drowned by his struggles and by the weight of the trap, for he can not survive under water very long without rising to the furface for a supply of air.

Water snakes can not do any damage to the large trout, but will certainly eat all the little fish they can get hold of. Even if they do no injury, they are not of any advantage, and may as well be disposed of.

Cray-fish very seldom eat the young fish. They will lie on the bottom, hidden in the mud, with the joint of the claw wide open and ready; then if any unfortunate troutling passes within reach, his doom is sealed. Crayfish do much more mischief by their burrowing propensities. They will make holes out of the pond, or from one pond to another, through which the water escapes, and very often the young fish also. The cray-fish is the scavenger of the water, and it may be a question whether a few of them will not do as much good, by disposing of decaying animal matter, as they do harm, by destroying a few fish; but they will eat spawn and the fry still encumbered with the sac. The greatest fear of all fish-raisers is that their fish will be stolen at night. A few old logs, stones and branches of trees strewn on the bottom of the pond, will make it impossible to drag the pond with a seine. Catching them by hook and line is the only means; and if the fish are well fed daily, it will take more time to catch a mess than thieves can usually spare.

Trout also find enemies in their own kind. The only way to stop them from feeding on each other is to give them plenty of other food. It may be as well, perhaps, not to feed them on small fish, unless these are chopped up fine, for the reason that trout soon accustom themselves to certain kinds of food, and will refuse anything strange. If they get into the habit of feeding on small fish, they will not be likely to make a distinction between trout and any other fish. Certain old trout also become unusually destructive to their brethren. Like the "rogue-elephants," and the "man-eaters," among the lions, they become morose and sullen, live apart from the rest, and make war upon everything around. When you find one of this kind, spear him at once, as there is no cure, and he will invariably destroy more than he is worth. It may be worth while to mention here how one trout eats another. An old trout will catch a smaller one, in some cases one-half of its own size, by the middle, and with its strong jaws hold it fast and swim around with it, while the prisoner worries and struggles to get free. This performance lasts until the victim gets loose or is exhausted, being continued sometimes for half a day. If the little fellow gets free, it is usually only to die a lingering death; for the breaking of the skin is fatal. When it is exhausted, the old rogue, dropping his victim, which until this time he has held by the middle, siezes it again by the head, and slowly swallows it whole; the operation sometimes taking several hours, and while in progress making the fish look as it had no head, but only a tail at each end.

In some localities minks are very destructive. These animals are particularly to be dreaded because they do not only kill what fish they want to eat, but will take out fifty or one hundred before they stop, and having found a well stocked pond, they will resort to it again and again. The best way to trap them is as follows: Make a box eighteen inches long by six inches broad and deep, leaving one end open, set a common game trap (such as used for catching muskrats) in the open end of the box in such a position that when the jaws are closed they will be in a line with the length of the trap. If it is set crossways it will be apt to throw the mink out instead of catching it. Put the bait in the further end of the box—a piece of meat or a dead fish will answer for bait—set the trap and cover it over with a large leaf. Now, there is only one way for the mink to get at the bait, which is by walking over the trap. Some trout-breeders also try to raise mink for profit as their skins are valuable; but their habits of eating fish and their custom of getting out of almost any box or yard in which they are confined do not make them agreeable neighbors for the trout.

The fish farmer can always tell by looking at his trout in the morning whether they have been disturbed during the night. If they have been molested, whether by birds, mink or men, they will appear excited and frightened. The water will be discolored by the mud which they stir up as they dart back and forth near the bottom, and the trout will be nearly all hidden under stones or in the moss.

Some writers on the subject of the diseases of trout have recommended the use of a salt water bath. The fish, when they are affected, whether old or young, are transferred to a tank into which salt is gradually introduced, and it is said that this treatment will cure fungus. It is a dangerous remedy, a sort of kill or cure, that in desperate straits may be resorted to, but such straits should never be permitted to arise. It will unquestionably kill parasites, but beyond that we have little faith in it. The large fish may occasionally be cured by rubbing with sand, but both of these are heroic measures. Although the fungus may be removed by the operation, it is almost certain to grow again, and usually more extensively than at first.

There is one kind of trout which we do not possess, of which we would very much like a specimen. We mean the trout which comes to dinner at the sound of a bell, or at the call or whistle of his feeder. Many writers about fish tell us to avoid all noises around the ponds lest they frighten the fish, and to be particularly careful never to fire a gun on the grounds lest the delicate ear of the trout should be too much affected. Trout cannot hear the sound of a bell, nor the voice of their feeder, nor even his whistle, neither will they stir one traction of an inch at the sound of a gun fired one foot above their heads; but the sight of a trout is very keen. His enemies are to be avoided by the aid of his eyes, and the trout starts and runs at every sudden motion, whether it is the shadow of the angler, or the falling of a leaf upon the water. He will be started by concussion, by a blow on the water, or a heavy step on the ground, but will mind no noise that is not accompanied with some demonstration that he can either see or feel. The angler may talk as loudly as he please, but he must approach the bank of the trout brook on tiptoe and hide behind any bush or tree. Fish are undoubtedly brought to the shore at dinner time by the ringing of a bell, but it is the motion, not the sound which attracts them. If the attendant will stand out of sight, he may ring till he is tired before his guests will put in an appearance.

OTHER FISH WITH TROUT.—It is not well to have other fish in the same pond with trout, they will probably destroy one another. Fish of any sort will eat the young of all kinds. Even the harmless and innocent looking goldfish will take young trout with a relish. A few sticklebacks will probably get into the ponds, but they will do no hurt unless they get among the babies two months old; the large trout will soon clear them out of their vicinity. Let the pollywogs wiggle their way in peace, and when they get to be frogs sell them or eat them.

Eels are exceedingly destructive in all waters to which they have access, and it is impossible to keep them out, as they can go up the perpendicular sides of water gates and possibly over the sides of the dam when wet with a heavy rain. The only plan is to use eel-pots and keep down their numbers as much as possible. They will follow the fry into the smallest rivulets, and on one occasion we saw an eel slash around in a little brook so as to stir up the mud and foul the water, that he might make sure of his prey which had become frightened and was trying to escape from him. He finds his food by sense of smell when the water is roily.

As for goldfish, in the year 1865 we had one hundred goldfish in a pond thirty feet long, twelve feet wide, and from four feet deep to shallow places three inches deep. We put 4,000 young brook trout in the pond, and in three days the goldfish had eaten every one of them. The little trout would hide themselves in the holes in the stone wall, where they were chased by the goldfish, which would lie at the hole for hours, watching for a trout; and when the trout made his appearance they would go for him as a cat does for a mouse.

CHAPTER VIII.

THE HOLTON AND OTHER HATCHING BOXES.

One of the most valuable, practical inventions in reference to the hatching of the eggs of the *salmonidae* was made by Marcellus Holton, while in the employ of the New York fishery commission. It consisted of a device for utilizing the upward flow of water among and through the eggs. It had been often noticed that trout sought as a favorite locality for depositing their eggs the parts of the bottom of the ponds or streams through which a spring made its way. Nature taught them thus, to secure a regular flow of clear, unpolluted water of even temperature, working its way between the gravel and eggs of which their nests were composed, and much larger percentage of the spawn deposited in such places hatched than when it was under any other natural conditions, for it was certain to receive precisely what it needed, a steady current of fresh and well aerated water, not increased or diminished in volume, not fouled by rains, not warmed by the sun or cooled by frost, and not bearing with it the germs of fungus or disease. Changes of temperature or condition are injurious to spawn, and by this plan, changes are avoided.

Holton in the arrangement of the hatching box which he invented, created an artificial spring of great volume, conveniently located and thoroughly under control. It was impossible to deposit the eggs over the natural springs, so the springs were brought into the hatching house. This was done by leading the water properly screened through a pipe into the bottom of a box, and allowing it to pass out over the top. A deflector was placed over the aperture in the bottom so as to break the current and distribute the flow equally in all directions, and trays were laid, one upon another in the box so that the water would have to rise through them all before it could escape, and the eggs being on these, must necessarily be kept directly under the influence of a steady but gentle and natural current.

These boxes were constructed especially for the incubation of white fish and shad eggs, although salmon, salmon trout, etc., can just as well be hatched with them. They are about twenty inches square and two feet deep, and will hold eighteen wire trays placed one upon another. The water enters from the bottom, passes up through the box, falls evenly into little troughs which run around the four sides, and is thence carried into a reservoir. The trays are lifted for cleaning by arms at two sides of the box fastened into a lower frame. The trays are made of wire cloth of so small a mesh that the eggs will not pass through, but large enough to permit the passage of the whitefish fry, which, as soon as they break the shell, are carried up by the current and into the reservoir, from which they may be taken out as required. Whitefish eggs placed in one layer will number sixty-four to the square inch. Each tray will hold about 18,000 eggs, and each box about 325,000. They can be made larger or smaller and will work equally well.

These boxes are the only device which will hatch whitefish thoroughly well, for whitefish are the most delicate and difficult to manipulate of all the salmon family. The eggs are much smaller than those of the trout and the fry are more tender than even the tender trout fry, which test the fish culturists best skill to raise satisfactorily. One especial advantage is, the difficulty that sediment of any kind finds in lodging upon the eggs. As it is carried upward, if at all by the current, it is swept along over the upper rim into the reservoir, and rarely catches upon the eggs. It has little opportunity to settle, and the number of eggs killed by this fruitful source of trouble is reduced to the minimum. Where the water passes from above down, it naturally deposits whatever it holds in suspension on its way, but by this reverse process, the sediment cannot fall, and cannot cling to what it touches, because it comes in contact with the underside. The aeration of the eggs is perfect, none are covered up by others so as to be shut out from the passing current and suffocated. In troughs the water strikes the body of eggs on the edge and then simply passes over and along them, not penetrating, but merely coming in contact with their surface; in the Holton box, the water enters every part, works up between every egg, and even if these are piled two or three deep, will vitalize all of them.

It must be remembered that impregnated eggs require the oxygen in the water as much as the living fry and will smother if shut out from it. Anything that does this, whether it be dirt, sediment, insufficient current or other eggs will destroy them and no plan has yet been invented which so absolutely prevents this danger. The economy of room is another important consideration where fish culture is to be prosecuted on a large scale. As we have said, eight boxes will contain and hatch two millions of white fish eggs, and an equal number of boxes of trout eggs will supply the place of a large establishment laid out in the old fashioned and ordinary method.

The openings through the wires are not round or square but a long narrow parallelogram, differing in width for the different sizes of eggs which are to be hatched. To understand this it is only necessary to suppose the wires stretched on the trays at proper distances from one another, and then bound together by cross wires at three-quarters of an inch from one another, or sufficiently near to hold all securely together. The wires for white fish eggs are nine to the inch; those for brook trout are eight to the inch; seven for salmon trout, and six and a half for salmon. In like way they can be adapted to any other species of fish that it is proposed to hatch. They could be used for shad where it is not desirable or convenient to use the regular shad box which is described in the chapter on shad hatching. For shad, the mesh of the trays is a little different being of heavier wire, square and twenty-two to the inch. These trays, it is unnecessary to say are painted with gas tar like the wood work of the troughs, and inside of the boxes and all other things with which the eggs come in contact. If the wires should not be, they would rust and the rust would penetrate and destroy every egg that touched it. The current may be caused by the natural flow of the water and by artificial means such as the use of a pump, and for shad and whitefish hatching, no trays are absolutely necessary. The boxes may be round or square and made of tin or wood.

We have said that whitefish work up through the trays and pass over the rim into the reservoirs. This is the habit with whitefish and with shad, but the salmon, salmon trout and brook trout, work down into the bottom of the boxes, and if the eggs are left in them until they are completely hatched the fry must be taken out when the trays are removed. There is some danger connected with this peculiarity, as the little fellows until the umbilical sac is absorbed, crowd together one upon another at the bottom, instinctively hiding from imaginary enemies, and will often get smothered. They can be drawn out by a syphon consisting of simply a piece of ordinary rubber pipe leading into a pail of water and will not be injured by the operation; or, if the fish are to be left in, a tin tube pierced with fine holes is put in the box and the upper end of the syphon led into that. However, the tin pipe where it enters the bottom of the box is usually constructed with a hole and a cork fitted to it, by means of which the fry can be drawn off and the box emptied.

The method of inspecting the eggs in this hatching box is as follows: Two wooden wedges are inserted, one on each side of the uprights attached to the bottom frame to hold them in place. One box is always left empty. The trays in the adjoining box are raised so as to bring the upper one just below the surface of the water and are wedged; this is examined, and after the dead eggs are removed it is placed in the empty box, lowered under water and wedged. When this is finished another is raised in the box which is being examined, and transferred after inspection to the other box. By wedging them each set of trays is kept in its place, and can be examined systematically. When they are all finished, that box is empty and may be cleaned if necessary. Then the trays in the next adjoining box are examined and transferred to it in the same way, and so on with one after the other till they are all completed and an empty box left at the further end of the row for use on the next occasion. If the water is pure this operation will not have to be performed more than once in two days, as the tendency of these boxes is to clean themselves and to prevent the retention of sediment.

By the use of the Holton boxes an immense condensation of room can be effected; each tray will hold more than ten thousand brook trout eggs, and the total number in each box will be about two hundred thousand. Our usual practice with trout eggs is to remove them from the boxes when they are about hatching and place them on the trays or gravel in the troughs where they will have more room, and can get out of their shells more readily. The empty shells will otherwise, sometimes clog the wires and stick to the embryos, unless the boxes are examined very frequently during the last stages of development.

GLASS JARS.—A pretty and ornamental modification of the Holton box, not essentially differing from it on principle, can be made by the use of glass, and will answer on a moderate scale. It consists of round glass jars filled with trays with the water entering at the bottom, which should be cast in the shape of a funnel to which is attached an India rubber pipe. The water passes out above through another pipe to the bottom of the next, and so on. The advantages claimed for this arrangement are the neatness, beauty and cleanliness, and the ease with which the eggs can be watched and studied at all times. It is well to have the supply pipe smaller than the connecting pipes between the jars, for fear of overflow in case of accidental obstruction, and from the first there should be a gradual descent, each jar standing a little lower than the one preceding it. When it is desirable to empty any jar it can be done with a tube of rubber used as a syphon, the supply of water being shut off. By drawing off the water into a basin, any young fish carried with it may be saved.

SELF-PICKER.—Another modification of the Holton box was made at the state establishment. It has been called a "self picker." It consists simply in removing all the trays and placing the piece of tin over the hole through which the water enters, which should be in the center of the bottom in such a way as to force the water to rise gently on all sides close to the edges. The box is shaped so that the sides converge towards this center and the water makes a moderate current along them upwards. The eggs which are placed loosely in the box are kept in a gentle bubbling or boiling motion by this arrangement. They are caught by the current, carried upward, and then dropping into an eddy, descend to be again whirled upward. When the fish hatch the general motion of the water is strong enough to carry the shells over the outlet, and it is manifest that by such an arrangement no sediment can at any time collect on the eggs. It was feared at first that the continual motion might wear through the shells. It has been used with trout, and is the proper arrangement if shad eggs are to be hatched in the Holton box, as for them trays are not necessary. If salmon or trout eggs are to be treated, a much smaller number must be put in each box, than if they were distributed on the trays. The original arrangement of the boxes is the best for general purposes, and these modifications, are only mentioned in case they should fit peculiar circumstances.

GLASS TRAYS.—It seems hardly necessary to refer to trays which have small glass tubes instead of wire netting on the bottom. These were among the first plans tried and will answer very well. But they are expensive to make and easy to break, while they are no better than our cheaper and stronger trays.

OUR PRACTICE.—A number of other arrangements could be detailed, but these are the best, and cover all conceivable circumstances. We have given so many that perhaps we had better state exactly what course we follow as the best, simplest, cheapest, easiest and most certain. We hatch whitefish in the Holton box, completing the operation there and allowing the fish to break their eggs, to work their way up through the wires, and pass over the upper rim into a reservoir, the egg shells going over at the same time. We have given up trying to feed whitefish and distribute them at once to the lakes they are to inhabit by depositing them in the water suitable for them.

Brook-trout, salmon-trout and salmon eggs we develop in the Holton boxes till they are about to burst their shells, then we place them on trays in the troughs. As they remain much longer in the boxes than in the troughs less room is needed in the latter than would be required if they were entirely hatched there. We give them a good current, and as soon as they are hatched and the egg shells removed, we spread gravel over the bottom of the troughs, or remove them to troughs with gravel on the bottom, as we believe they are more contented, so long as the umbilical sac remains, if they can hide their heads, or imagine that they are hid between the stones. We observe that if they are kept at this stage in bare troughs they are uneasy and keep struggling about from place to place. Just before the sac is absorbed we watch them carefully, especially the brooktrout, to prevent their crowding on one another, and when they do so they are removed in a broad flat net from the head of the trough where they congregate to the lower end, or are otherwise spread out. This is done at night as well as during the day when there is a large number together. As soon as the sac is absorbed we remove the gravel and keep them in clean troughs with nothing in them to catch or conceal dirt. We again increase the current and feed the young six times a day on liver comminuted to the utmost possible degree, and diluted with water. We distribute the fry as soon as possible thereafter, and put them in the smallest spring runs connected with the streams or ponds they are to stock, and not directly into the ponds or streams themselves.

CHAPTER IX.

MANIPULATING SALMON AND TROUT.

Spawning Season.—The salmon family of the Atlantic States, including the eastern salmon, the salmon trout, the brook trout, the whitefish, and the lake herring, spawns in the autumn and fore part of winter. The grayling spawns in March and April, the California salmon in summer, commencing in the latter part of August, and the California mountain trout in Spring, beginning in the middle of March. Trout commence to spawn about October. The colder the climate is, the earlier they will spawn. In Caledonia Creek the trout lay their first eggs about the 12th of October; the water standing then at about forty-eight degrees. In the preserves where the temperature, at that time, is a few degrees higher, they begin to spawn about the 1st of November, and cease about the 1st of March. The length of the spawning season depends upon the equality of the temperature of the water. In streams where the temperature does not vary much, winter or summer, the length of the season is three or four months, sometimes more, and in cold mountain streams it only lasts two months, closing by the middle of January.

Signs of Spawning.—As the season of spawning approaches, the difference of sexes shows more clearly. It is very hard in the summer to tell the difference between a male and female trout. By handling them much and watching them closely the trout breeder comes to know the male and female apart almost instinctively; but he would be puzzled to tell just *how* he knows it. The male is generally sharper jawed than the female at any season of the year, and lines drawn from his shoulders to his tail would be straight without any bulge in the middle, while the female has a rounder jaw, and even in summer is more protuberant in the middle. These are general signs, and by no means universal. It is only in the spawning season that difference of the sexes can be told with any certainty. As this season approaches the distinctions become more marked. The difference in size is one peculiarity, as the eggs grow large and fill the belly of the female. It will not do to mistake food for eggs. A trout recently gorged with food looks just like a female full of eggs; but the food soon disappears, as a trout is an animal of quick digestion, while the swelling caused by the maturing eggs gets larger as the spawning season approaches. The colors of the fish, also, are at that time a guide. The female turns to a dark and sombre hue, while the colors of the males grow very brilliant, a line of brilliant scarlet red often developing itself along his sides on the edge of the belly.

NATURAL SPAWNING.—As the spawning season approaches, the trout seek places in the creek adapted to the purpose. These places have a pebbly bottom in shallow water close to the spring or head waters of the creek. Trout will work their way up over the shallows of a stream clear to the source; but if there are springs in the bottom which is the case with almost all creeks they will invariably spawn there, without going up farther, or if they find a shallow place with gentle current and gravel bottom anywhere in the creek, they will use it. Very few of the eggs laid in such a place will come to maturity unless there happens to be a spring. The males sometimes go up the stream first. At this season the males engage in fierce contests for the possession of the females.

These battles often end in death to one or both of the combatants. That these battles are fierce, the deep wounds left on the dead bodies of the slain will bear witness. They have been known to fight for two days, and then both be killed. However, when they are once mated the battles cease and the pair are hardly ever seriously interfered with. Intruders in any quantity come around, seemingly out of curiosity; but, no matter what their size, they leave as soon as the husband, for the time being, darts at them. These intruders are, perhaps, waiting for a chance to devour some of the stray eggs which the female drops. The male and female being paired, go to the chosen place. They lie side by side together when not disturbed; but the male is occupied most of the time in driving off interlopers. It is very curious to see a little male with a big female in charge. Usually the little trout clears the way for the large one without a show of resistance. In the ponds when the trout are fed the largest get the meat while the little ones get out of the way, and swim to the further side of the pond, and even if the meat is thrown where they are they will not take it until they have waited to see whether it is not the pleasure of the big fellows to claim it. At the spawning season all this is changed, they will attack a trout three times their size if he comes within less than a respectful distance of the female. Often while the male is driving off one, another on the opposite side will make tender advances; quick as a dart the proper husband returns to chase the gay deceiver. In fact his time is fully occupied with chasing off intruders. If they are too numerous the female will dart from the nest over which she hovers, to help her chosen mate. A nest is made in the gravel by the female. It is simply a shallow hole about six or eight inches in diameter and about two or three inches deep. This is made by diving down at intervals against the gravel and as she comes up giving it a *slirt* to one side with her tail. Nearly the same motion as may be often observed when trout dart down to the bottom and rub their sides against it to free themselves from parasites. The dipping motion is continued for some days until the nest is large enough to suit her. After lying over this some time the female is ready to emit a portion of her eggs. The male lies by her side while she does so. However busy he may have been in driving off interlopers, he seems to know by instinct when the female is ready to emit her eggs and is always by he side. At the time she emits her eggs he emits his milt over them. They do this with a curious curl upward, which every trout-breeder should see for himself. Very often the male and female lock jaws together and their heads slowly rise, apparently trembling with excitement. They emit eggs and milt until a nearly vertical position is gained, still lying over the hole, then, they fall away from one another and the male retires to some secluded spot where he remains five or ten minutes resting. This interval the female employs in covering her eggs. She will *flirt* in with her tail all the stones of proper size to be found near her nest, and if there are not enough to cover it to her liking she will go above, and, picking out a particular stone, work it down backward between the two ventral fins. This labor she continues until the eggs are completely covered.

After five or ten minutes the male pays her a visit to see how she is getting along. He looks around a little, eats a few of the eggs if he can find any uncovered, and then retires to his lurking place again, where he remains twenty minutes with only occasional visits to the female before he recovers from the exhaustion which he has undergone. The female does not seem to rest, she continues covering the eggs and does not then leave the place. The reason for this is that she has not yet emitted all her eggs, for trout occupy some time in their spawning, laying their eggs at intervals, as they become ripe. Observers differ as to the length of time occupied in spawning. The time is not usually more than three days, although sometimes extending to six days, the female covering the eggs as she emits them.

When it is understood that some of the eggs do not sink into the nest, but are carried off by the current, and that only a part of every batch escape the jaws of their parents, and of the many trout swimming around the spawning place, one may begin to preceive the advantage of artificial methods. To make the danger of loss greater; after the nest is finished, the parents gone, and the eggs nicely hatching, another pair come along intent on similar business. The female sees the place where the first has laid her eggs, and, fancying it a good spot for her own nest, begins to make one there. As soon as the eggs are uncovered, by the preparatory operations, the pair eat up all they can find, and then proceed to lay their own eggs, only perhaps, to be served in the same way by others. When it is considered, also, that all kinds of water-fowl are fond of these eggs and diligently search after them, and that in the spring time the young fry furnish a large proportion of food for the older ones, the wonder seems to be, not that there are so few trout in our streams, but that there are any left. Another cause of the rapid diminution of trout in settled countries, is the tame ducks which are allowed on the stream. They wander at will peacefully up and down the stream, explore every foot of the bottom, turning over the gravel with their long bills, and leaving very few of the eggs to hatch.

NUMBER OF EGGS.—The number of spawn which a trout will give has been variously estimated. They commence spawning at two years old if well fed and large. It has been asserted that eggs have been taken from a trout one year old, or rather taken in the winter of the same year in which it was hatched. This may be so, but it is more interesting in a physiological point of view than for any practical purpose, as there are so few that it is not worth while to take them. A trout two years old will give from two hundred to five hundred eggs, a three year old from five hundred to one thousand eggs, a four or five year old from one thousand to two thousand eggs. ' This is only an approximation, as the number of spawn depends upon the weight and health of the fish, and not on its age. In some cases the number of eggs is much greater, but four thousand is the most we have ever seen taken from one trout. In estimating the number of spawn from a given number of fish in a pond, it must be remembered that some are barren, and some diseased, and some, perhaps, will not go up into the race. So that the average yield of two and three year olds, females only counted, will not be over five hundred, of four and five year olds, not over one thousand each.

The proportion of males to females in a pond should be about one half. Not so many are necessary to fecundate the eggs, and it would be an advantage in one way to have fewer, since then there would not be so much fighting in choosing partners, and as all the females do not spawn at once, one male would be enough to serve several females; but, on the other hand, the males seem to run out of milt before the females get through laying their eggs, and towards the close of the season it is often difficult to obtain males with milt enough to fecundate the eggs; so that it seems better to have in the pond an equal number of males and females, thereby giving more chance of saving some of the milt till the last of the season. The males are very amorous and will pair again and again. It very often happens that some of them die from the exhausting effects of the season. The best way is to have an equal number of males and females, everything considered.

TAKING SPAWN BY HAND.—The trout will not spawn in the ponds where the bottom consists of large stones or weeds; but if there is sand or gravel anywhere on the bottom of the ponds they will spawn on it: Therefore be careful to have only the raceway, where the water enters, covered with gravel. In October this may be washed and cleaned from the weeds which will have grown in it during the year. As soon as the fish are ready to spawn they will ascend from the ponds into the raceway seeking a place to nest. Then they are ready to be taken out and the spawn expressed. At the entrance of the raceway there should be grooves to receive a frame on which is tacked a net of coarse bagging about eight or ten feet long. One corner of this bag should be narrowed, left unsewn, and tied with a string, like the mouth of a meal sack. The race should be covered over in spawning time, as the fish will come under the cover better and are not so likely to be frightened by any one passing. If there are fifteen hundred or two thousand fish in the pond the net may be used every day in the height of the season, and when the fish become scarce, once in two or three days.

Indications of spawning having been observed, the covers are put on the races, and as soon as there are fish in the raceway, the net is gathered up in one hand and the frame held in the other, in such a position as to be put in the grooves as quickly as possible, so as to let none of the fish escape from the race. Go quietly to the spot, and do not walk down the raceway to get to it, but approach from one side and put the net in the groove as quickly as you can. The water running down will swell the net out to its full length. The covers may be then removed, and with a stick you may frighten the fish down from the head of the raceway into the net. As soon as they are all in, the frame may be lifted out of the water, and the fish are then enclosed in the bag. A tub of water should be previously brought near the spot, and the end of the net can be lifted into the tub and untied, when the fish will all fall into the tub without trouble. Coarse cloth is better for the purpose than netting, as it can be more easily tacked to the frame, does not hurt the fish so much, and lasts longer; besides, the water swells it out and holds it open for the fish to run in better than it would a net, and the fish not seeing you through the cloth as they would through an open mesh, are not scared, and do not try to run back up the race.

It must be remembered in this and all subsequent handling of the fish, that if the outer skin of a trout is broken or abraded by the hand or in contact with any hard substance, it will, in nineteen cases out of twenty, cause the fish to die. A white fungus appears on it first where the skin is broken; this fungus spreads over the fish until it is sometimes half covered with it before it dies. We speak of the covering of trout as "skin," because it feels like it and looks like it, although in reality trout are covered with minute scales. They will get over a deep and clear cut much more quickly than over a bruise where the cuticle or skin only is broken.

The fish being now in the tub must be taken to the hatching house as quickly as possible. There are probably in the tub some fifteen or twenty fish, and all the operations must be conducted as quickly as possible so that they will not die in the small quantity of water to which they are confined. So long as the fish lie quiet in the bottom of the tub there is sufficient air in the water to sustain them, but as soon as they begin to come to the surface and try to leap out, it is a sign that the air is nearly exhausted and the water should be renewed. They will also open their mouths wide, just as a person would when gasping for air. The question has sometimes been asked how long a trout would live out of water; the answer is, about as long as a man would live under the water. Trout will die in a tub out of which the oxygen has been exhausted by their breathing, more quickly than they would die in a cloudy day if out of the water entirely.

A fire may be made in the hatching-house to warm your fingers, which will probably get cool while engaged in this operation. A six quart milk-pan is to be provided, if you have many fish, and also another tub of water, into which to put the fish after they are deprived of their spawn. Select a fish, and holding it over the milk pan, which has been dipped in water to wet it, rub it gently with the fore finger and thumb, from the pectoral fins to the vent. A little experience will show how this is to be done. If the fish is ripe, a few drops of pearly colored milt, or orange hued eggs, will be forcibly expressed into the pan. If the milt is not of this color, it shows that the milt is not good, and another male must be taken and treated in a similar manner. The female must be pressed more slowly and oftener than the male. If the eggs are not ripe, by passing the hand lightly over the belly, you will feel them beneath, hard, like shot. In that case put the fish back into the pond, for the eggs to ripen. When the eggs are ripe, the belly will be soft and flabby, and the eggs beneath the skin feel loose and change their position at the touch. So loose are they, that by holding the fish in a horizontal position, and then moving it up and down, the eggs will change, and fall downwards or upwards as if in a bottle. The operation must be continued until the fish are emptied of eggs and milt. The eggs in the pan may, at intervals, be gently stirred by moving the pan; this is to change the position of the eggs, so as to be sure that all come in contact with the milt, and when the operation is completed a half-pint of water is poured on them and the pan set in one of the hatching troughs through which the water is running; this will keep the eggs up to the proper temperature, and prevent a sudden change when they are transferred to the trough. The eggs will now agglutinate or stick to the pan, and to each other, for a little while.

In handling the fish, gentleness is essential. A trout, it is well known, may be tickled under the belly, and rather seems to like it, and will lie quiet in your hand while your are doing it. By putting the hand quietly in the water, moving it cautiously around the fish, and gently lifting him he may be raised high and dry, and will lie quietly without a struggle. There is a way of grasping a trout firmly, but gently, so that he cannot squirm, and yet not hard enough to break the skin.

We give a cut of handling a large fish which shows the proper position, except that the fish had to be held too high from the pan in order to get a good photograph of the operation, and that the operator is left handed.

SETH GREEN TAKING SPAWN FROM A SALMON TROUT.
THE PROPER POSITION.

The fish must be grasped by the head, if you are right-handed, with the right hand, and by the tail, or rather the lower part of the body, with the other hand, and held over the pan with the belly near the bottom of the pan. As soon as the fish is quiet, the right hand may be gently slipped down from the head, and the fore finger and thumb used to press the belly. The fish still being held by the tail, and lower part in the left hand, and partly supported, perhaps, by the sleeve of the coat, or by the bare arm, and the remaining fingers of the right hand. Every one will have a way in which he can do this best, and will find it out after a few trials. If the fish is large and struggles violently, the usual direction given in the books, is to let an assistant hold the head. We counsel you, if the fish struggles violently, whether it be large or small, to drop it back into the tub, manipulate another, and after a few minutes try it again; it will lie quiet after a while. If you attempt to hold a fish, which struggles violently, you will be very apt to kill it. It, in addition to your own two hands, you get the two hands of an assistant on the struggling fish, there is not much chance of saving him alive. A better way is to file the barb off of a No. 4 hook, then tie it with three feet of line to a pliant switch three feet long. Hook your fish on this, through the jaw, and holding it in a tub of water, let it struggle until it is exhausted. Then the hook can be slipped out, no injury having been done to the trout, which can be handled without difficulty.

The large trout are harder to handle, struggle more violently, and are more apt to be killed than the smaller ones and do not average so many eggs, although now and then one will have a very large number. Therefore, we consider that the best fish for breeders, when the operation is conducted by hand, are those weighing from one-quarter of a pound to one pound.

The pan should be elevated at one side, during the operation of taking the spawn, by standing it on a block half an inch thick, and enough water will drip from the fish so that by tilting and shaking it the milt can be brought in contact with the eggs. Formerly it was the custom to half fill the pan with water, but now the eggs are mixed as dry as they can be, and it is found that a far higher percentage are impregnated. The milt seems to drown in water quickly. Only enough eggs should be taken to cover the bottom of the pan with a single layer. If more eggs are to be had, more pans should be used, and as soon as all the fish have been handled they should be returned to the water.

It takes very little milt to impregnate a large number of eggs; but, in practice, we generally take all the milt we can get out of the haul. It is sometimes our custom also to put the male fish, whose milt has been exhausted, into a pond by themselves, to keep them from running up into the race again and troubling the females. This is a very good plan, if you have plenty of ponds and plenty of fish. If you have but a small number of males compared with the number of females, put them back again into the pond, as they will probably have a second and third renewal of milt.

After stripping a female once she should be returned to the tub from which she was taken, and should be stripped again after a short time during which other fish are being handled. This is to get the last egg from her, and if it is not done a few will remain and she will go on the spawning beds to deposit them as if she had a full supply. If she is cleaned entirely she will not bother herself or her owner about the matter again that season. The California mountain trout retain their eggs and milt with more determination than our brook trout and must be humored like a cow that will not give down her milk to any one but the creature for which nature intended it. After the trout are handled they are returned to different tubs according to their sizes, as this is the occasion that we take for sorting them, and then they are returned to their proper ponds.

Twenty to twenty-five minutes having now elapsed since the pan of eggs was set in the trough, gently tip up the pan. If the eggs are loose and roll separately as you move it, they are ready for subsequent operations; if not yet loose, let them remain a while longer.

The semen of the male is full of *spermatazoa* or animalcules. These will live for ten or fifteen minutes in water; dry, they will live six hours. There is a hole for the reception of these sperms in each egg. The egg always sinks into the water with this hole at the top. It receives one of the animalcules only by this opening, which then closes. There seems to be a special arrangement of Providence that the eggs shall agglutinate— stick fast to each other and to everything they touch— so that they shall not float away until they are impregnated and the trout has had time to cover them. In the eggs of other fish, such as bass and perch, the same arrangement is seen; only they stick fast the moment they touch anything, and stay there until hatched out, while the substance that fastens the eggs of the trout dissolves as soon as the mother has had time to protect them.

The eggs will now be loose and lying on the bottom of the pan. Pour off the dirty water until only sufficient is left to cover the eggs. If this is done very gently, the eggs, although very light, will remain at the bottom, as they are somewhat heavier than water; then sink the pan into the water, at the same time tipping it as described in the chapter on "Eggs," and take it half full of watre. The influx of water will wash the eggs around somewhat, and dilute the dirty water remaining in the pan. This is to be poured off, as before, and the operation repeated, until the water looks perfectly clear. There will be some dirt and droppings of the trout still left, which can be carefully picked out with the nippers. If an egg should happen to be broken, while being taken from the trout, every vestige of it should be carefully removed, as the slimy, sticky contents will get on the other eggs and kill them. The eggs are now ready to be placed in the trough, and having previously raised the water in the nest to which you wish to transfer them, by placing a strip across proceed as described in the chapter on "Eggs."

From the above description, it will be seen that a few lessons in artificial impregnation, from an experienced hand, will probably save the beginner much time and money. A written description of the process, however good, can never take the place of verbal instruction; partly because it never conveys exactly the same idea to all, partly because seeing a thing is better than hearing about it, and mostly because a written description is a general one, and hardly ever tells of the minutiæ and variations which constantly occur in practice. As an example of this, it has been urged, all through this book, that in moving the eggs the beginner should not touch them with the feather, but should move the water over them, so that the eggs should follow the current thus created; also that he should be very careful, in removing the dead eggs, not to touch the others with the nippers. But, we constantly move the *eggs* with the feather, and push to one side the sound eggs with the nippers, in order to get at the dead ones. The reason simply is, that long practice has given the *knack* of doing it, without injury to the eggs, that a tyro does not possess.

In every process of the management and handling of eggs we have urged the greatest care and delicacy. Others however, claim that a rougher treatment will answer equally well and save much trouble. We give the following method adopted by Mr. Wilmot of Canada, as a specimen case. He says: "I have adopted a new plan this year, and I have found it to answer admirably, and infinitely better than the one I have practiced hitherto. I formerly practiced the same system that I allude to, namely, taking the eggs from the fish and putting the milt upon them, and then allowing them to remain twenty or thirty minutes. The system I have adopted this year, I think, will be conclusive in itself as showing the benefit that we have derived from it and the amount of labor saved. The system that I have adopted is this: we take the female fish out of the water and strip her as rapidly as possible; perhaps two or three fish are taken out one after the other, so that in some instances we will have nearly a gallon of eggs—a half of a gallon any way, or three-fourths of a gallon—in one vessel. We then take the male fish and begin stripping him in a like manner to get the milt. An attendant is standing immediately alongside of the other gentleman who is manipulating. He has a measure which is calculated to hold a thousand or two thousand, as the case may be, and he stands immediately alongside and dips these eggs out as rapidly as possible and puts them on the breeding-tray, and the breeding-tray is put in the hatching-trough. In that way I have impregnated a larger number of eggs by far than I have in the last seven years in which I have been engaged in this work. It is simple in itself, and so different from what has hitherto been practiced, that I thought it advisable to mention it here, because it is so much better than any other system I know of."

This manipulation requires that the eggs should be ladled directly into dry trays and handled quite roughly. It may answer for salmon, but is not the practice that we recommend, either for them or for trout. There is more trouble in our method, but the results we are confident, are correspondingly superior.

DEAD OVA.—The following is taken from the Ohio Report on fisheries, as it expresses our views on the possibilities and limits of impregnating the eggs of dead fish:

An opinion has long been prevalent that the roe or ova of a dead female fish could be fertilized by milt taken from a dead male fish; in other words, it was firmly believed that the ova taken from the dead fish, as they were opened and the entrails removed at the fish packing-houses in Sandusky, became fertilized by the milt from dead males when their entrails were removed and all cast into a common heap as offal, mingling with the ova of the females, and that then and there the ova became as thoroughly fertilized or impregnated as if both the fish were alive. Many otherwise intelligent and well-informed persons very freely asserted that during the winter months thousands of millions of young whitefish "just out of the egg" were to be seen around about the wharves of the packing-houses in Sandusky bay.

Believing it to be of the utmost importance in artificial reproduction of fishes to know with absolute certainty whether the ova of a dead fish can be fertilized, Mr. Charles Carpenter, of Kelley's Island, was instructed to institute a series of experiments to determine this matter beyond any peradventure. He was instructed to obtain both the milt and ova of fishes dead one hour and those dead several hours, and subject them to the process of fertilization; then with the milt of the dead male to fertilize the ova of a live female; then with the milt of the live male to fertilize the ova of a dead female; finally, to preserve the milt of a live fish and fertilize ova directly after extrusion, with the milt, after it had been taken six, twelve, eighteen, to twenty-four hours from the male.

The results of the fertilizing experiments is to the effect that *immediately* after the death of the fish, male or female, the ova, under favorable circumstances, can be fertilized; that the milt can be preserved some hours without losing *all* its fertilizing power; that milt of fish within an hour after its death will fertilize almost as well as that taken from a live fish. These experiments were made with whitefish (*coregonus alba*) milt and ova—those of other species may differ widely in susceptibility of impregnation or fertilization after the death of the parent Statements are made that milt of the *trout* kind has been shipped from California to Boston without parting with its fertilizing influence entirely.

Mr. Carpenter learned, furthermore, that when a single drop or two of milt was all that could be obtained, and it appeared thickish, that the fish was about exhausted and such milt contained conparatively few spermatozoa—hence it was almost worthless for the purpose for which it was intended. But when the milt was in considerable quantity and was very fluid, then it contained comparatively the maximum quantity of spermatozoa, and a single drop of it would fertilize more ova than twenty drops of the thick. Both milt and ova were entirely worthless if exposed to a temperature below 31°. This degree of temperature appears to deprive the milt of its fertilizing influences, and deadens the susceptability of the ova of being fertilized.

Many statements are made by fishermen and others to the effect that the eggs of fishes are often found frozen in ice on the shore or banks of streams, as well as ponds and lakes, and afterwards hatched successfully.

Some experiments, carefully conducted by Mr. Carpenter, demonstrate that whenever the eggs are subjected to a temperature below 32° Fahrenheit, that vitality ceases.

Statements have been found going the rounds of the press, to the effect that fish have been found in the streams, frozen stiff, and afterwards restored to life. All experiments made in this direction have resulted in the absolute death of the subjects of the experiments. Experiments made by us in fertilizing eggs after they were extruded, resulted in showing that where five minutes were allowed to elapse after the eggs were obtained, and before the milt was applied, only four per cent. were impregnated, and of all those that were left a longer time none were impregnated.

CHAPTER X.

GENERAL REMARKS ON TROUT BREEDING.

There are other methods of hatching the eggs which are partly natural and partly artificial, and which persons can use who are not in condition to oversee the eggs during their long period of incubation. Frames of wood have been built over a raceway made from springs, and on them gravel has been placed. The strips or slats of the frame were wide enough apart for the eggs to fall through into the lower part of the raceway, which was closed at the lower end so as to force the water up among the gravel. The frame was set at such a depth as to give a couple of inches over the gravel, and more or less under the frame. The fish were allowed to spawn by themselves, covers being laid on to protect them from disturbance. The eggs fell through the slats as they were impregnated, and hatched below where nothing could get at them. This yields a moderate percentage, and will work better than if the gravel is laid on six inches thick, so deep that the eggs are retained in it and cannot fall through.

Another plan was to place a double set of trays or screens, the lower one of such fine wire that the eggs will not pass through; that is, of about ten or fourteen threads to the inch. This wire is attached to a frame, made of inch stuff, and another inch strip nailed above it. The upper frame is of the same width and length, but the sides are from three to four inches deep; upon this a coarse screen, of three or four wires to the inch, is fastened. The fine screen is first laid in the race, which being made of proper width, it fills, and the coarse screen is laid over it, with the wire side down. There is a space, between the two screens, of one inch, protected from invasion on the top and bottom by the wire screens, and on all the sides by the inch strip of the small screen. The top screen, which has sides three or four inches deep, is then to be filled with coarse gravel, so coarse that it will not pass through the meshes, to the depth of two inches. This gravel will overcome the buoyancy of the wooden frames, and cause them to sink in the water. Now the screens are ready for use.

A trout comes along, and finds the gravel. She sees no screens—only some nice gravel for nest-building, in what appears to be a shallow box. Suspecting no evil, she proceeds to make her nest, and in the process of "slirting out" gravel with her tail, she moves it away from the meshes of the coarse screen, and leaves the bottom of her nest an open network. On this she emits her eggs, which are at the same time fecundated by the emission of the milt of the male trout lying by her side. The eggs fall down into the nest, but pass through the coarse wire screen, and are caught by the fine meshes of the lower screen. There they are safe. The trout covers up the hole as usual. The hangers-on find no eggs to devour, and go their way. Another trout may make her nest in the same place, without disturbing the eggs already laid, safe in their resting-place. Here they may be left to hatch, or you may take a pan of water, and taking off the upper screen, gradually lift up the lower screen, brushing the eggs to one corner with a feather, and tip them all at last into your pan without having exposed a single egg to the atmosphere, without any trouble in handling the fish, and without any loss of the breeders.

These screens may be made as wide as your raceway, if it is not over two or three feet, and of a square shape. If your raceway is four feet wide, it is better to have your screens each two feet square, as this size is most convenient to handle when they are filled with gravel. Enough of them can be placed in the raceway to fill its whole length. One thing requires to be noted here. It takes a much larger raceway, for this process of natural impregnation, than it does when the eggs are impregnated artificially. In the latter case you need only room enough to make one trout after another *believe* she is going to lay her eggs; in the other you must have room enough for her to carry out her intentions. This is known as the Ainsworth screen, and was invented by Stephen H. Ainsworth.

Much discussion has taken place among fish-breeders and others interested in the art, as to the comparative value of the two methods, aside from the manual labor and loss of fish involved. That is, by which of the two methods the most eggs are impregnated, and which are the most healthy or will produce the best fish. In answer to the first question, we say that a skillful workman will impregnate more by hand than are impregnated in the natural way. To the second question, we answer, that the fish hatched from eggs rightly impregnated by hand, are just as strong, grow as fast, and live as long as the others.

STOCKING PONDS.—The question is often asked by beginners, with what shall I commence fish-farming? Shall I buy the eggs and try to raise them, and wait three years for full-grown fish, or shall I buy adult fish, and from them take eggs? The answer to this question depends upon two circumstances. First, how much money you have; and second, how long you wish to wait. It is much cheaper to buy the eggs than the adult fish; but then you will have to wait two or three years before you have any breeders. The wisest and safest plan would be to try a few thousand eggs, and also a few hundred two-year old fish. Ten thousand eggs would cost thirty dollars, and two hundred two-year olds would cost about forty dollars. Two hundred two-year olds would probably give about twenty thousand eggs. If you take this advice, you will have eggs to experiment with the first year. With care, you will hatch out more or less, but in any case your experience will be invaluable to you for the next year, and you will have a stock of breeders, to furnish eggs, as you want them.

STOCKING STREAMS.—Persons who own trout-streams would very often like to have them re-stocked, and some make feeble attempts to do it, by putting in a few thousand young fish. This would re stock a small stream, if it were done every year, for some years. But it is folly to suppose that a large stream which has been fished for years, and thousands taken from it every year, can be re-stocked *quickly* by putting in a few hundred, or even a few thousand young. If you attempt to stock your streams at all, don't do it half-way. Remember that the less fish you put in, the longer you will have to wait. It is much easier to stock a stream than to raise fish in ponds; because the young fish will take care of themselves better than any one can take care of them; and if they are protected from danger, until they are forty-five days old, they are then tolerably able to look out for themselves. In stocking a stream, the young fish should be taken to its head-waters, or put into the springs, or little rivulets, which empty into it. As they grow larger, they will gradually settle down stream, and run up again to the head-waters in winter to spawn.

When putting fish into a stream, do not put them suddenly into water much warmer than that of the vessel in which they are brought. They will not so likely be injured by putting them into colder water; but try to avoid all sudden changes, and gradually raise or lower the temperature of the water in which you bring them, until it is even with that of the stream in which they are to be placed. —Remember that it will be two years before you can hope to sell any fish for table use; so do not enter into the business unless you have some means of support for that time. The persons who have the most natural advantages for this business are those farmers, who have springs or cold streams on their farm—now almost useless—but which may be turned to advantage in raising fish. They, depending on their farm meanwhile for support, can give time and attention to the experiment, and engage in it altogether if it succeeds, or abandon it, without serious loss, if they fail. It is peculiarly adapted to them, also, because it demands most attention in the winter, when they have least to do on the farm. Meanwhile, it would be well for impecunious young men, seeking fortunes, to leave the business to capitalists and corporations.

To those who wish to raise fish for their own table use, or to afford sport in angling, we would say that we can think of no way in which a little time and money can be so well laid out as in trout-raising.

A prejudice existed in the public mind for a time against raising brook trout for public waters. This was regarded as interfering with private trout breeders and tending rather to the encouragement of sporting than to the increase of the supply of fish food. But this prejudice has been overcome. The advantages of some healthful and exhilarating out door amusement are pressing themselves more and more upon a nation of hard working men, who are confined day after day, and often half the nights, at the desk or in the counting room, and who suffer to so large a degree from paralysis and softening of the brain. All work and no play has been found not only to make Jack a dull, but a sickly and miserable boy. Our ancestors had in a thinly settled country as much physical labor as their bodies needed, but their descendants are suffering for the want of out door exercise.

Nor is this all. Perhaps in no branch of fish culture are the results more immediate and more apparent in the mere return of food than in brook trout culture. Innumerable inland streams that were once inhabited by trout are now wholly depleted and denuded, not only of that kind of fish, but of all others. They are bright, sparkling, noisy, like some men and utterly empty. They make an instantaneous and wonderful return for restocking. Fry placed in them are absolutely safe. There are no enemies to threaten their existence. They have the whole water to themselves without even a parasite to bother them. Food is abundant, for it has been increasing for years, and they not only live in security, but grow with rapidity. In the year 1875, the State of New York directed its Commissioners to purchase a trout breeding establishment, and to raise and distribute brook trout. Since then some million and a half have been hatched yearly, and many streams have been replenished. In every instance the results have been most gratifying. It would seem almost as though every fish lived and increased in size steadily, till he was caught. Those that were taken first were small of course, those that were left had the more food and by next year yielded nearly as much in weight although fewer in numbers, as the first. The following year the fish were still larger and without allowing anything for the natural increase, furnished a splendid return for the first investment.

This addition to the yield of any stream is so apparent as to convince the most skeptical. It is not to be disputed or gainsayed, and those who have once visited a trout stream the year after it has been stocked and have seen the young fish then from three to five inches long darting out at every step from under weeds and roots for the entire length of the stream, will need no further proof that trout culture is eminently practical. In such cases you may almost say that the number taken from a stream will depend simply upon the number you put in, while the cost of hatching and transporting them is as nothing compared with the yield of pleasure and profit. No brook that has once contained trout need any longer be without a good supply of them. Shad and salmon go to the sea, and when they return only swell the natural yield which varies at best and is influenced by other causes, so the direct effect is not clearly seen. Whitefish and salmon trout are almost lost in our vast lakes and rivers, but brook trout remain where they are placed, grow and are caught among the residents of the neighborhood, and contribute directly to the support and amusement of the people. Streams that have been wholly worthless in producing food are once more replenished and are often rendered a very valuable adjunct to a farm or country place. Trout will always bring a good price in market, and the farmer who has a good trout stream or pond on his place can rent the fishing to advantage if he does not care to keep it for himself, and as population increases such fishing privileges will become more and more valuable.

TRANSPORTING LIVE FISH.—Many expensive tanks have been constructed for transporting fish alive, answering the purpose more or less perfectly. We give here a simple and inexpensive method: Take a barrel or cask, washed until it is clean and sweet. Fit a cover to it tightly to prevent the water splashing over while on the cars or wagon. A piece of canvass tied over the top, answers every purpose. A hole one inch in diameter may be made in the middle of the cover. Fill with water within six inches of the top, as the agitation of the water on the journey helps to aerate it. Tie some ice in a piece of flannel and fasten it to the side of the cask near the top so that it shall not swing about and bruise the fish, and the cold drip from the ice will sink to the bottom. If the journey is to be a prolonged one, fit the nozzle of a common bellows with a tin tube long enough to reach to the bottom of the cask, and by blowing a little now and then the fish can be carried thousands of miles. We do not give this as the best plan, but as a cheap and inexpensive method answering a very good purpose. The best apparatus would be a metal tank of some kind with double walls, permanent ice chamber in the middle, and automatic air-pump.

Young whitefish are in condition to transport from the first to the tenth of February; salmon trout from the tenth to the thirtieth; brook trout from February twentieth to April fifteenth and should be put in the small spring rivulets one and two feet wide, that supply the main stream. No man, while transporting fish, should go to sleep and allow them to be left alone while in the cans, as it will be sure death to them. A man may think he knows all about carrying fish, because he has carried a few minnows in a pail for fishing; but he will fail sure if he does not follow the directions to the letter. Six twelve-gallon cans filled with fish is all one man can take care of.

We use, ordinarily, the common milk cans, and have found them to answer. The water is aerated when fresh cannot be got by being poured from one bucket to another, held some distance apart. The older the fish, the more frequent changes of water they will need. In order to do this when traveling by railroad the water is drawn off by the syphon; make a tube $2\frac{1}{2}$ inches in diameter as long as the can, cover the bottom and 6 inches up the tube with wire lining and put the syphon in it when the water is drawn off. Draw the water as low as is safe, just before reaching the station, when fresh water can be turned in from the pump, or drawn from a hydrant. A milk can will hold about 7,000 whitefish fry, or 5,000 brook-trout fry, or 4,000 salmon-trout fry, according to the length of the journey and opportunities of changing the water. They will carry only about fifteen full grown fish of any species.

All fish should be deposited as near the head of a lake as possible, that they may not go into the outlet before they become familiar with the waters. The young fish should be deposited during the night when most large fish do not feed, and will find hiding places before morning. They can be transported much more easily and safely in cold weather than in warm.

In all operations with fish eggs we cannot too strongly impress on our readers the necessity for the utmost care in handling. Fish eggs are different from birds eggs and often have a tough tenacious skin, but they are as easily killed by rough usage as the shell of the smallest bird is easily broken by a fall. They should be moved and touched with the utmost delicacy, and never except on necessary occasions. It would be better if they had a thin shell, for then persons would more quickly see the fatal results of any carelessness.

MR. PALMER'S METHOD.—Mr. Palmer, one of the most successful fish culturists of the West, has kindly furnished us the following communication describing his method of growing trout which differs a little from that in general use. He recommends the use of zinc troughs, but we doubt whether that metal would answer in all waters which might when loaded with certain substances have a chemical effect upon them that would be deleterious to the eggs. However, under his management and in his location they answer well:

For hatching of trout and salmon, I prefer zinc lined troughs, they are easily kept clean, and the fish are where they are wanted until they exhaust the food sac. While I can not hatch as many in this way as with the Brackett tray, or Holton box, I think I can hatch healthier fish.

My hatching troughs are twelve feet long and eighteen inches wide, and I hatch from fifty to eighty thousand to the trough. I run the water about an inch deep over them, and let on all the water I can without washing the eggs off.

I cleanse my water by settling it in deep boxes before it goes on the eggs. For the last ten or twelve years my trout fry have been remarkably healthy, prior to that I had lost them by tens of thousands, and think that the cleanliness and simplicity of the process has much to do with their health. My experience, not alone around my own ponds, but with others that I had occasion to visit, is that the longer trout are confined or domesticated the healthier their progeny becomes, and in this connection I would say that this applies to their pisciverousness or canibalism, I have one pond in which I have trout from two to eighteen inches long, and never see one devour another. Taming them for generations seems to take away their wild voracious nature; of course I would not recommend the raising of different ages together, and think when mixed together, if neglected, they would return to their old practice of living off one another.

Every trout breeder knows that the difficult stage with them is from the time they absorb their sac to the time they get to feeding well, and much of the trouble is to get them to eat.

Some ten years ago in my perplexity to find something that they would eat, I thought I would try a little sweet cream. Well, it floated off like oil, and I said to myself that "any fool might have known that," and set down the cream and went to thinking again. Next morning I went out, and whilst standing at the head of the trough thinking what I would prepare them for breakfast, I picked up the cream, which had frozen over night, and dropped a little in, and to my surprise it broke up into little fine particles, much like cornmeal, and floated on the water, and I had the satisfaction to see the little fellows grab it. Since then I have fed my fry with it for about two weeks, then mixed it with liver, and finally came to all liver. I think the secret of their taking to cream so kindly is that it is so easily swallowed, and have often watched my young fry struggling, straining and gasping, trying to swallow the smallest particles of meat.

I sell trout eggs at four dollars a thousand, and the young fish at eight dollars a thousand when they absorb the sac, and add eight dollars a thousand each month that I keep them. After that find I that this ratio brings them, when ready for the table, to about fifty cents a pound, the price at which I sell trout for the table.

I have land-locked Atlantic and Pacific salmon, and crosses between the Pacific salmon and the trout, but would not recommend them for pond culture. The trout will make much greater growth on the same food than they will, and do much better. I sell them at half the price of trout but never get an order duplicated.

I feed livers, melts, kidneys, and sometimes lungs of animals that I pay the butchers two and a half cents a pound for, yet my fish do not cost me as much pound for pound, as the beef and pork I raise. The reason is that I keep my ponds well stocked with insect-food. I would rather lose the use of one or two ponds at the head of the stream, and devote them to insect breeding, than to have the insect food fail, as by this means I not only raise my fish cheaper but get a better fish than those who feed exclusively prepared food.

Please excuse my tediousness in this description; I think fish culture worth a good deal of talk.

Yours,

A. PALMER.

FISHWAYS.—The selection of a proper form of fishway is a difficult matter, and has never yet been determined. Several forms and plans have been selected, from the plain, open, inclined shute to a system of compartments divided from one another and stopping the water by obstructions. Fish will pass up these, even shad, which are among the most timid, but the results bear little comparison to what would take place with an open river and free access to the waters alone. Many fish never find the mouth of the pass, and others are afraid to ascend it. By a law passed in 1874, by the New York Legislature, the commissioners were required to cause to be constructed in the upper aqueduct, in the town of Niskayuna, Schenectady county, a "Brewer's Patent Chute and Fishway." This direction of the legislature was not founded on any act, declaration or advice of the Commissioners, and there was no discretion left them or called for by the act in question. They were to make the contract and see to the proper execution of the work, which they did. The work was well and reasonably done, and while declining yet to express a positive opinion in a matter of such doubt and uncertainty, we have been favorably impressed with the working of the fishway, and hope it will prove what has been so long sought without complete success, an easy and moderately expensive method of overcoming obstructions in a river, either placed there by nature or by man, and which form an insurmountable obstacle to the ascent of fish.

This fishway is twenty (20) feet wide between piers or side walls, its lineal distance is forty-one (41) feet, height of dam five (5) feet, incline one (1) foot in ten. The passage-way for fish is eighteen (18) inches wide by fifteen (15) inches deep. There are six (6) angles, three (3) on each side; and built of timber, stone and iron.

Brewer's Improved Chute and Fishway was patented April 30, 1872, and the contract had to be awarded to J. D. Brewer. This work was pronounced by those present at the opening, to be an entire success. The inventor and contractor in presence of at least twenty gentlemen, with a round scoop net of thirteen inches in diameter, took out two fish at a haul, two thirds of the way up the ascent, and numbers of the fish were taken in the fishway when they were going up. As soon as the coffer dam at the upper end was taken away the roily water rushed down the fishway; the fish, thinking that there was a flood, rushed up. Some were taken with a scoop net nearly at the top of the dam.

IMPROVING STREAMS.—Where a person has a small stream on his place which is adapted for trout, but is not large enough to accommodate many, or grow them to a good size, it can, at very small expense, be made a considerable source of pleasure and profit. All that has to be done is, to dig small ponds or long, narrow holes, say three or four rods long, and five feet deep, and throw some logs or brush in them. If possible, lay the logs crosswise near the bottom, in order to have the water work under them and make a clean "scour." Then all that has to be done is to place some trout fry in the brook above the ponds. As the fish grow they will settle down into the ponds where they can find shelter and safety, and whence they can be taken with a hook and line whenever they are wanted; the danger of fouling around the brushwood being an additional excitement to the angler. The fish need not be fed, as food sufficient will accumulate upon the logs and brush.

CHAPTER XI.

OTHER VARIETIES.

GRAYLING.—Before passing to the consideration of other kinds of fish, we desire to speak of species allied to the salmon and trout, although different in many of their habits.

Much excitement was created in the year 1873 among ichthyologists, by the discovery in some of the streams of the state of Michigan, of a variety of fish not previously supposed to exist in the United States, called the grayling. The grayling is a much esteemed European fish, common on the continent and in certain streams of England. It is a good sporting fish and excellent for the table, and as it spawns in a different season of the year from trout, it furnishes food and sport at a time when trout cannot be killed or eaten. The existence of such a variety might be of great benefit to the older states if its acclimation was possible and it should prove as well adapted to eastern waters as to those of the state of Michigan.

Mr. Seth Green proceeded to Michigan in the spring of 1874. So little was known of the habits of the fish that he arrived after the spawning season was nearly closed. On the 30th of April he reached the Au Sable river where they are supposed to be most abundant, although they are known to exist in all the streams of that region. The weather was still very cold and much difficulty was experienced in effecting the purpose of the expedition. The water of the river was found to be forty degrees Fahrenheit, but the air at that time ranged from sixteen to twenty degrees. Finding that the spawning season was over, Mr. Green dug up some impregnated eggs which had been deposited in the natural method, and capturing some living fish, left on his way back with eighty large grayling in eight twelve gallon milk cans, and one hundred and six eggs. He arrived at Caledonia on the 6th of May, with the loss of one dead fish and two fatally injured. From conversations had with trappers and hunters, it is supposed that grayling are found in the Au Sable, Manistee, Muskegon, Boardman, Au Gray, Rifle, Marquette and Cheboygan; in the latter in company with the brook trout. The latter fact would go to confirm the impression that grayling would live in our trout streams.

The adult grayling were placed at first in a pond with a small water supply. Here they did not seem to do very well and were soon transfered to another pond which had a strong current. In this they recovered, but preferred to lie at the head of the pond and in the quickest current. They soon became tame and mixed with the brook trout without being molested. They were fed the same food and treated in all respects as the brook trout.

The eggs, one hundred and six in number, were hatched out in the same way as the eggs of the brook trout; their incubation taking about the same time. The young fish looked at first like the whitefish; but the young grayling is larger and has a larger sac than the white fish, though smaller than the brook trout. They took food very readily and though it was very neat work at first to feed them, after they had grown a little they gave no trouble. There is no doubt that they can be raised artifically, but the question remains whether that is worth while. They are more delicate to handle, require as much care and must have equally difficult conditions.

When first hatched they lie on the bottom like young trout, but commence to swim on the third or fourth day.

May 5—Eggs arrived from Michigan.
" 8—First egg hatched.
" 11—All eggs hatched out; one lost.
" 12—First fish began to rise and eat.
" 15—All swimming.

The eggs are nearly as large as trout eggs, but of less specific gravity. The fry resemble the young of the whitefish. They were about three inches long in December. Of the value of the discovery the future only can determine, but some excellent results may still flow from this undertaking. These are the first and only grayling ever hatched artifically. Up to the present time, however, March 1879, the grayling have exhibited no desire to spawn, and do not enter the raceway for that purpose. What they would do if turned out free in our eastern streams we cannot say, but when kept in confinement they will not spawn with us, and hence are useless to the fish culturist, whatever they may yet prove to be to the sportsman.

BLUE BACKED TROUT—*Salmo Oquossa.*—This fish which is a species of char or *salmo umbla* of Europe, has only been noticed heretofore in some of the lakes of Maine, although varieties of char are found in most of the waters of Canada and the far north. Its characteristic peculiarities were pointed out some years ago by Girard, who conferred on it its name after the original Indian title of the lake in which it is found, now known as the Rangeley. Although it is very like the trout in appearance, wanting only the distinctive scarlet or carmine specks, in habits it is quite dissimilar. It passes most of the year in the deep water, only coming to shore in October, and invariably at the same day to spawn. It then appears in countless numbers and crowds all the inlets and outlets of the lake. It remains only until the act of reproduction is complete when it returns to its ordinary resting place.

Its meat is said to be excellent and it is certainly very prolific. It is supposed to be the principal food of the brook trout of that region which attain the enormous weight of eight or ten pounds, the largest reached by any of the true brook trout in America.

A few of these fish have been lately sold in New York market. Before that they had not been an article of commerce, nor much prized as a delicacy even by the inhabitants of the country where they dwelt.

Its first dorsal fin is higher and narrower than that of the trout, its caudal is more forked and its sides have no carmine or vermillion specks, but instead large yellow spots which become a pale blue after the fish has been kept some time out of water. It makes its appearance in the outlets and inlets of the lake on the tenth day of October, when it comes up to spawn. It is punctual in its yearly re-appearance for that purpose to the very day, and the inhabitants expect to draw much of their winter supplies of smoked and salted fish from its hordes. It averages from seven to nine inches in length—never more, and in weight three to four ounces.

In 1874 the Fishery Commissioners of Maine succeeded in obtaining 30,000 of the eggs of this variety, and as they had more than they needed, 5,000 of them were purchased for our state. We regret to say they did not reach the state hatching house in very good condition, nearly a thousand dying on the way or the day after their arrival. Some hundreds of them however, hatched out.

We have reason to believe that the blue backed trout is found in Oregon, and possibly in some of the lakes of Northern California, but its culture artificially, will not probably prove profitable.

SMELT.—These fish which are a variety of the salmonoids are to be treated very differently from the trout and salmon, for their eggs are exceedingly adhesive. They ascend the rivers in early spring. In the neighborhood of New York they are caught largely in the Raritan and Passaic rivers.

About five miles above the city of New Brunswick there is a dam which blocks the river, and which the smelt cannot surmount. The fishing grounds, extend from the old wooden city bridge down the river for two or more miles; very little, if any fishing being done above the bridge, on account partially of the little depth of the water, partially because the smelt appear to pass down the river again, after being impeded in their onward course by the dam. The smelt are caught entirely with seines, which include in their sweep, nearly the entire breadth of the river, averaging about thirty rods.

The seines vary from thirty to sixty fathoms in length, one hundred and eighty to three hundred and sixty feet, and are about fifteen feet in breadth, with meshes one-half inch square. The time of working the seines depends much upon the state of the weather and the water, but as a rule, the fishermen are engaged early in the morning and again in the afternoon.

The smelt spawn throughout the month of March, the eggs are small and so adhesive that they must be deposited upon the trays where they are to remain. There are about forty thousand eggs to each medium-sized fish, and they will hatch in about a month with a temperature of water of from thirty-five degrees to forty degrees, or in the ordinary water in the river in about eighteen days. The spawning fish, as fast as captured, should be placed in tubs, or, if not ripe, they may be kept in ponds till the eggs mature. When they are to be handled a tray dipped in water should be placed in a tin pan without any water in it. The eggs are stripped directly on the tray, and the milt, as soon thereafter as possible, then a little water should be added, just enough to cover the tray, and the whole shaken about till the eggs are evenly distributed. A few minutes expire before they adhere finally, but when adhesion once takes place they must remain undisturbed till they hatch. The time of development is so short that there is no trouble in their management, and they may be hatched in unlimited numbers. The spawners may be stripped directly into a shad hatching box and that left in the current of the river, and a large number hatched in an ordinary fish car, in which the parents had been confined to mature their eggs and in which they had spawned of themselves. The trays are removed to the hatching boxes after the eggs have adhered by the hardening of the mucous matter that surrounds them and then treated like trout eggs except that the dead fish cannot be removed.

WHITEFISH.—We have received the following communication on the hatching and raising of whitefish. No one has had greater experience or success with this peculiarly delicate and difficult variety of fish than the writer, and whatever he says on the subject may be regarded as authority:

MADISON, WIS., JUNE 22d, 1878.

Dear Sir:

My experience in hatching whitefish, *coregonus albus*, is that the first and most important thing to insure perfect success is to get the eggs well impregnated.

2d—To use great care in transporting them from the fisheries to the hatchery.

3d—To give them a good circulation of water.

4th—To use lake water or water of same temperature.

5th—To employ sufficient help to remove all dead or unimpregnated eggs every day for the first thirty days after they are placed in the hatching boxes, after that time, once in two or three days is quite sufficient,

Now, in taking and impregnating the spawn, I use two men ; while one handles the female the other handles the male, and I find by so doing we have but a small percentage of unimpregnated eggs to remove, while by using both at the same time we follow nature as nearly as it can be done artificially. We have to transport the spawn of the whitefish for our hatchery from one to two hundred miles. We use what is termed the dry process for transporting them, having an attendant constantly with them to handle the boxes very carefully whenever it becomes necessary to move them at any time while *en route* to their destination.

I also take great pains to get the temperature of the spawn in the boxes equal to the water in the hatchery before placing them in their proper place in the hatching boxes.

I use the Holton Patent Hatching Box which I consider the only proper appliance for hatching whitefish to insure a genuine success, all others that I have seen or heard of have been a failure to a greater or less extent. I use plenty of water running through the boxes to cause enough current to nearly lift the eggs from the trays, or, in other words, I use as much as possible without lifting them. I use the water from Lake Michigan, the same being pumped directly from the lake into the hatchery, therefore we have the same temperature of water that the spawn have that is deposited naturally by the fish in the lake, which I consider necessary to produce good healthy fish, such as will thrive and prosper. In fact my experience in hatching this variety of fish in spring water and also in lake water has convinced be that those hatched in spring water come out prematurely and cannot survive more than a short time.

I find it also necessary to remove all the unimpregnated eggs as soon as possible, also to wash and cleanse them from every particle of glutinous matter, after which I have no trouble with their matting or sticking to the trays and then by using due diligence to business I never fail, and success crowns all my efforts. I have also been experimenting in feeding a few of the whitefish of the last two season's hatchings and have succeeded in keeping some forty of the hatch of 1877 until the present time which now measure from six to seven inches in length. I also have about the same number from this year's hatch which are growing finely, and are in better condition and more thrifty than those of last season were at their age which is no doubt owing to the improvement in feeding, which we have made since last season. The great trouble in raising whitefish artificially, is in teaching them to feed which requires both patience and perseverence. We commence when the fry are from ten to twelve days old. We use the blood of veal or beef mixed with sweet milk or cream, and water enough to make it as thin as water itself which is done by taking a small quantity of the blood into a dish with about the same quantity of cream or twice the quantity of sweet milk, and then stirring it thoroughly; after it has become well mixed, we then commence adding water and continue to add the same until the whole has the appearance of roily water, when it is ready for use. We then pour into the trough at the upper end so that the current will carry it down the entire length and give the fry ample time and opportunity to partake of the food.

The first positive indications we have that they are feeding is the unusual excitement which is shown by their continually darting hither and thither through the roily substance. In a short time you can discern in them a marked difference in the color of the body, which loses transparency and becomes dark. After the fry have been feeding a few days we dispense with the cream or milk and use only water for thining the blood. When two months old they will take liver ground fine using water in the same manner as with the blood. When a few months old they take the ground liver prepared in the same way you prepare it for young trout. Care should be taken not to feed any food in lumps as they seem to choke easily, in fact the only fish we have lost of those of the hatch of 1877 in six months past, three in number, have choked to death with careless feeding. They become nearly as ravenous feeders as the trout, rising and taking their food near the surface and also picking it from the bottom which is covered with fine sand kept clean and free from decomposed food.

I have no doubt those I have been feeding the past fourteen months would take the hook as readily as the trout of the same age.

Yours truly,
H. W. WELSHER,
Supt. Wisconsin Fish Com.

CHAPTER XII.
SHAD CULTURE.

The fish for cultivation in American waters, the fish which nature has given us preeminently as one of its best gifts to man is the shad. Adapted to all our seaboard streams; once numerous in every river that emptied into the ocean, from Florida to Maine; prolific to a remarkable degree, easily manipulated, requiring no aid to procure its support, it fairly cries to man for his assistance and protection. An excellent addition to the table, it is welcome to the epicure, while so cheap has it been within the memory of even young men, that it was not denied to the poorest among us. Of course it has been growing scarce of late; inroads have been made on its vast numbers. The fishermen with their drift nets and seines and stake nets, of which there must be thousands upon thousands of miles in the entire country, have done their best in the way of extermination, and have almost succeeded. Some streams have been depopulated, in others fisheries have ceased to be remuncrative; the markets are being scantily supplied, and prices have risen enormously. Shad are following in the wake of salmon in consequence of American energy of destruction. A few years more of uncontrolled pursuit and shad would have been as rare as salmon, and selling for a dollar a pound. The want of legal restrictions, the neglect of restoration, or even preservation would in a very short time have deprived the community of what is still, in a semi-exhausted condition, a large part of its fish food.

HABITS OF SHAD.—Shad make their appearance along the Atlantic coast of the United States early in the year. The first school usually strikes in at the Florida rivers in

February, and is succeeded by other schools which enter the streams further north, as the season advances and the temperature of the water increases. It was for a long time supposed that immense shoals of herring, shad and other migratory fishes traversed the ocean in certain circuits, sending off divisions at all convenient spots, the main body keeping on its course, and these smaller armies filling and utilizing for spawning purposes the various rivers adapted to their wants, no more being sent to each than would be necessary. These voyages were even thought to extend across the ocean and possibly even around the entire globe, and it was supposed that the shad and herring which visited Europe were a portion of the same vast body which skirted the coast of the United States of America. Investigation has tended to break down this theory, and it is now generally abandoned. It was found that over fishing in certain streams diminished the yield of such streams without affecting others that were better preserved or more neglected. This would not have been the case if the supply came from one central source from which all rivers were equally furnished, and to deplete one stream would only lead to a general diminution. So far from this result being attained, however, the rivers of Florida were as crowded as ever while the fisheries of the Hudson and Connecticut were almost at an end. The converse of this experience was reached when efforts were made to improve the supply of certain streams. The artificial culture of shad in the Connecticut and the Hudson, under the fishery commissions of those States, has improved the yield in those rivers to a marked extent, without having any effect on that of streams further south or north. A few shad may have wandered into the Hudson from the Connecticut, or *vice versa*, or may possibly have strayed even further, but the benefits of the shad-hatching operations were practically confined to the waters in which they were practiced, and in those waters were proportioned to the extent to which such operations were carried.

Experiments made with salmon in Europe clearly established the proposition, as far as these fish were concerned, that they always returned as mature fish, after their sojourn in the ocean, to the rivers in which they were hatched and from which they emigrated when young. They were marked in various ways usually by cutting off the adipose second dorsal fin while in the smolt stage, when they were preparing to descend to the sea; and it was found that they invariably returned to their breeding places, except in a few instances, which might safely be attributed to accident. Their residence in the salt water being short, these experiments were easily made, and as the fisheries were mainly in private hands, and under close supervision, the results could be obtained with accuracy. Another discovery was made in the same connection by the deep-sea fishing, to the effect that these same salmon did not roam over distant portions of the ocean, or even descend to great depths, but remained near the mouths of the rivers to which they belonged.

Shad remain much longer in the ocean, requiring three and four years to become mature, although the males probably reappear a year earlier than the females; but there is every reason to believe that the same rule governs their motions that applies to the migrations of the salmon. It may, therefore, be concluded that shad do not roam about the "vasty deep" in immense shoals, making journeys of thousands of miles, and sending off relays to each river whose mouth they pass, but that they remain quietly near the streams where they are bred till the time comes for them to leave the ocean, seek the fresh water and complete their duties of procreation. No migratory tribe of fishes can accomplish the round of its life duties in one element; it may live and grow in the sea, but cannot breed there; while although it must breed and may live in the fresh water, it will not attain its full proportions in that element alone. Instinct, which could hardly teach them how many of their number to direct to any given stream before they had explored it, could and does inform them when the proper time of year has arrived for them to deposit their eggs. The temperature of the water and the heat of the sun are their guides, in exact accordance with which will their appearance in the streams take place, occurring first in the more southern and gradually succeeding in those to the north. It cannot be doubted that a sensible diminution of the entire shad supply of this continent has taken place within the last fifty years, and were this drawn from one body it would be natural to expect that while the rivers first reached by the school would be filled as they originally were, those last in order would be left utterly bare. In such case the school coming from the south would send off their full quota to the streams of Florida, Georgia, South and North Carolina, until the entire body was exhausted, and those of the New England or middle States were left with no fish whatever. Such, however, is not the fact, and it is only those streams where man takes more than his proper proportion that are being gradually depopulated.

When the mature shad prepare to perform the duty of propogating their race they direct their energies to that, and without intermission. They seem to be pressed by an overpowering necessity, and will do their best to overcome all obstacles that nature or art may have placed in their way, and they never rest until they have reached their proper spawning grounds.

With all this class of fish, it is essential that the breeders should reach the upper waters of the rivers, where alone they can spawn and hatch their young. Were a dam or any impassable obstruction placed across the river for a single season, the entire yield of that year would cease, and a new supply would have to be obtained.

Shad being a migratory fish, spend the greater part of their time in the sea where they find their food, for, like most migratory fish, they do not feed in the fresh water; there they prey on shell fish or other small creatures, which, while inexhaustible in number are wholly useless directly to man. In February, March and April, May, June and July, urged by the re-productive instinct they ascend into the fresh water to deposit their eggs. Unlike salmon however, they do not go far up our rivers nor require special conditions of locality or temperature to complete the procreative art successfully. They seek out some rocky ledge where there is a gentle current, and uniting in pairs press their vents together and extrude the spawn and milt in a spasm of amatory pleasure. They build no nests, the act of spawning is performed while the loving pair are in rapid motion—so rapid that they often spring out of water and their fluttering along its surface is clearly distinguishable. Their only precaution against predatory animals is that they spawn at night. The eggs are left to themselves to the mercy of their enemies and to fate. The parents, as soon as they are through this duty of their existence return lean and wasted to the ocean to recuperate and enjoy themselves.

Here is incredible wastefulness; countless creeping, crawling and swimming creatures live upon those same eggs. These sneaking enemies search the bottom and pry into every cranny and crevice for them. Their hunger is unsatiable and their energy untiring. But, injurious as they are other dangers are more destructive. A little increase of current will wash nine-tenths of the eggs off the rocky ledge into the muddy flats where they perish for want of aeration. A heavy rain will roil the water, and on its subsidence there will be deposited upon the eggs a thin covering of sediment which will destroy them all absolutely and without exception. Eggs of fish in order to hatch must be continually surrounded with fresh water; they require the oxygen of changing water just as land animals require the oxygen of changing atmosphere. Shut a man in a small room, or a mouse under a glass jar, and as soon as he shall have exhausted the vitality of the air in the confined space he will die. Fish and their eggs can be smothered in precisely the same way. A muddy deposit upon eggs excludes aeration and death ensues to a certainty. There is no exception to this rule, and this is the most fatal peril to which shad spawn is exposed and which annually decimates the yield of young fish.

So great are these risks that shad could never have held their own were it not for the compensation of their wonderful fecundity. They produce ten thousand eggs to each pound of weight, which is ten times as many as salmon or trout and it is not unusual to obtain sixty thousand eggs from a single mature female. This is their protection, that among the vast number laid some will hatch, and although the per centage is small the aggregate has been large enough to maintain the supply. But here arises the most serious trouble when man interferes with the established order of nature. Accident sweeps away just such a proportion, the water and land creatures which feed on the eggs will abate no jot or

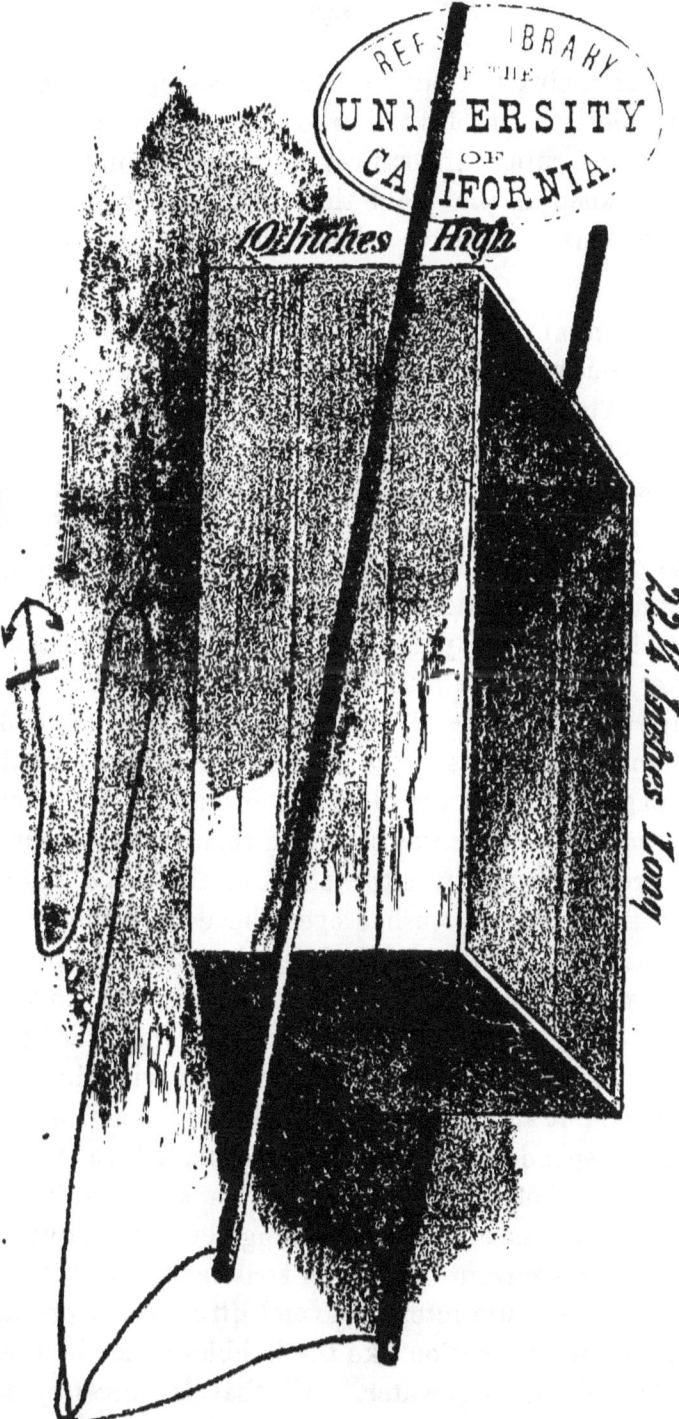

SHAD HATCHING BOX.—(LONG FLOAT.)

tittle of their exactions, so when man steps in he upsets the scale and tumbles the whole shad fishery into confusion and ruin. It requires a greater annual contribution to keep up the yield than with trout; it falls off proportionately greater when this contribution is cut down.

ARTIFICIAL METHOD.—Shad eggs differ essentially from trout eggs and require wholly different manipulation. They are much smaller and lighter. If a trout or salmon egg is dropped into water it sinks at once to the bottom, but a shad egg will almost float, and has but little more specific gravity that the water itself. Shad eggs are less than half the size of trout eggs and require as their best condition for hatching a temperature of from sixty-five to seventy-five degrees. They will hatch at a lower temperature but in such cases mature slowly, while eighty degrees of heat is as much as they can endure. When experiments were first made in their artificial propagation they were placed in ordinary trout troughs and much trouble was found in their management. If a current of water was turned on to the same extent as with trout they all washed over the end of the troughs, while if the supply was diminished so that they retained their places they died of suffocation. It was only after many different devices had been tried that the proper invention was discovered—a simple box with the bottom knocked out and replaced by a wire gauze netting. This box is suspended by floats of wood nailed on the sides so that the bottom is presented at an angle to the current, the degree of inclination being determined by the velocity of the current. The water striking against the screen enters the minute interstices, and lifting the eggs keeps them in gentle motion like the bubbles of air in a pot of moderately boiling water. All that is necessary is to attach these boxes one behind the other in a long row, anchor them in the river and fill them with impregnated spawn and the work is done. The continuous motion of the water passing around each egg and holding it suspended aerates it perfectly and makes its hatching a certainty. Hardly one per cent. of healthy eggs fail to hatch, and while the process is going on hardly any care or attention is required. Fish and eels cannot enter the boxes to prey, nor can the eggs be driven out by the water, and lost.

In the artificial manipulation of shad the parents are taken in seines from their spawning beds. The haul is made at night, at which time only can ripe fish be found in any considerable number. The captured fish are thrown indiscriminately into a boat and are stripped at once as they die quickly. They are afterwards sold in the markets. The eggs, which are caught in a pan with a little water in it after being allowed to stand for a few minutes until impregnation is complete, which is signified by their swelling in size and reducing the temperature of the water some ten degrees, are poured into the hatching boxes and left to themselves. Nothing more is required. In twenty four hours the black eyes of the young fry will be visible through the shell, and in from three to ten days they will be hatched. So rapid, simple and inexpensive is the process of shad culture. There are no flannel screens to be washed and cleaned every day or two as with salmon or trout; no rows of troughs to be examined laboriously with benumbed hands in winter weather; no weary waiting for months with every hour filled with danger; no contagious diseases or spreading conferva to be guarded against; no careful superintendence without which failure threatens; no particular selection of water or locality. The boxes are merely anchored in the stream, tied one to the other, the eggs are turned in by the hundred thousand, and in about a week there are myriads of minute but lively shad swimming about and begging to be allowed to grow fat and feed mankind. The eggs are as a score to one in abundance; the loss is almost nothing, and the time, trouble and expense are infinitely less.

Nor is this all. When the trout is hatched he is encumbered with his umbilical sac for a month to such a degree as to be unable to protect himself, while the shad can be turned loose the day he is born. It is true that he has the same appendage, but it is a small one and does not seriously impede his motions. In habits also the shad fry exhibit their superiority over their more aristocratic cousins. Instead of seeking to hide their diminutive heads under every leaf and pebble, and in every out of the way corner playing at hide and seek with death, they with greater wisdom push out into the deeper water and broader stream. There in mid-river they float heading up against the current, taking the water with whatever of microcosmal food—invisible to man—it may contain into their mouths, feebly wagging their limp tails to keep them in position, and slowly settling down stream toward the ocean where they are destined to pass the next year or two waxing plump and fat for the benefit of man, but at no expense to him of purse, brain or muscle.

The discovery of the habits of shad fry was made in rather a singular way and exemplifies the dangers to which in their natural condition they are exposed. As with their hatching, so with their treatment afterwards; it was natural to follow the system we understood and practiced with trout. The box containing the first results of the fish culturist's skill was towed near the land

and some of the fry ladled out into the river. Instantly a crowd of minnows, killey fish, dace, chubs, shiners and all manner of small fishes swarmed from all directions and proceeded to devour their still smaller brethren. They arrived with astounding swiftness and in incredible numbers. Had a dinner bell been rung it could not have summoned a larger or hungrier congregation. In a minute not a shad remained alive to tell the tale; they had gone to the realm of the departed; they had entered within the veil; they had sought the bourne from which no traveler returns. In other words, they were in the rapacious maws of a lot of little worthless fish which could do much harm but no good to any one. From the stomach of a little shiner not over an inch long, which was caught with a dip net, seventeen young shad were taken.

By this time it had become apparent that something was wrong, so the rest of the hatching was temporarily deposited in a small pond built of sand and pebbles on the shore of the river, while their case was taken under serious consideration. Next morning it was at first thought they had all escaped for they were not to be found anywhere in the body of the pond, but were finally discovered at its outer edge. A long narrow pond projecting into the river was then built, and pieces of white paper placed on the bottom so that the diminutive creatures could be more easily watched. Next morning they were again found crowded at the outer extremity. The problem was solved. Instinct had taught them to seek the deep water where their insignificance was their protection. Hardly a half inch in length and not more than a pin's thickness in breadth, they would escape unnoticed the monsters of three, four and five pounds weight which roamed about in the main current, while the terrors of the mighty deep would keep away their far more dangerous enemies of an inch or two in size. The big fish would not see them and the little ones could not follow them.

HANDLING THE EGGS.—Shad do not spawn during the day, but commence these operations about dusk and continue them till midnight. For the purposes of artificial cultivation they must be taken when they are perfectly ripe, as it is called, in other words when the eggs are mature and ready to be deposited in the natural way. So it is that over these beds, and during the first half of the night, the seines are swept to catch the spawners and milters which are to be manipulated scientifically, as they are thus secured in their best condition. The moment the seine is hauled, its contents of all sorts are ladled with a scoop net into a boat, and while it is being set again the fish are handled. The manipulator has in front of him on one of the thwarts a tin pan containing a little water, and taking fish after fish he holds it over this with one hand and gently presses its belly with the other. The ready performance of this is a matter of practice, and if the eggs and milt are ripe they will exude under a slight pressure. As fast as the fish have been stripped, males and females being used indiscriminately, they are thrown into another boat.

When the fish have all been stripped or the pan is full, it is kept in gentle motion for thirty minutes, after which the water is changed, and the gentle motion and changing of the water alternated until the eggs swell, become hard and distended, and the impregnation is perfected.

In the course of the first fifteen minutes the temperature of the water in the pan falls some ten degrees, and the eggs finally become so hard that they feel to the touch like shot; although when first dropped into the pan they can hardly be felt at all. This is repeated as often as the net is hauled, and when no more spawners can be caught, the pans are carried to the hatching boxes and emptied into them. These boxes are covered with coal tar, to prevent the wire rusting on the bottom and the growth of animal matter, and have along the sides sticks of wood acting as floats, and presenting the wire screen at such an angle to the current that the eggs are kept in a perpetual boiling motion. The boxes are fastened one behind the other by ropes attached to the floats, and need little or no care except to be occasionally stirred at slack tide. The screens on the bottom have a square mesh and twenty-two wires to the inch. The eggs exhibit life in twenty-four hours, and hatch in from four to ten days, according to the heat of the water, and then the living fish are turned out and left to care for themselves. The only precaution taken being to turn them out at night when their enemies are not feeding and they can have time to get into the deep water.

Instead of trusting to good fortune to get ripe spawners from the nets these may be obtained in a way similar to the treatment of salmon and trout. A pond may be built by damming up a stream running into the main river, in this the shad may be confined till they are ripe. It has been supposed that shad were so timid a fish that they would hardly ascend fish-ways, and could not be kept in confinement, but such does not turn out to be the case. There is no difficulty in ponding them and in examining them from time to time till they become in proper condition to strip. They are not more timid than other fish.

The cultivation of shad is necessarily a work of public duty, it cannot be maintained by private enterprise as the increase belongs to the entire community, not to any individual. This may be a communistic possession of property but even that is better than no property at all. It is an easy and simple branch of fish culture and were it assisted by proper laws and the breeding fish allowed to reach their spawning grounds in sufficient numbers its results would be astonishing. As it is, the more fish that are bred the more fishing is done and the closer is drawn the barrier that shuts them out from the upper waters of the rivers that they inhabit. At least forty-eight hours in every week should be a close time during which no fishing should be allowed in order that a fair proportion at least should be permitted to fulfil the duties and necessities of their continued existence. No skill in fish culture can hatch fish when there are no parents from whom to obtain the eggs. That proposition is self evident.

MIGRATORY FISH CONFINED TO FRESH WATER.—An experiment was made by Mr. Wilmot of Canada, by which it is thought to be proved that salmon can live in fresh water wholly, if they are permitted to migrate forward and back from the great lakes into their fluvial tributaries. This change, it is claimed, satisfies the demands of their natures and supplies them with abundant and fitting food. A similar conclusion appears to be reached in reference to the shad. A number of the fry were deposited in the Genesee river, and were seen in that and Lake Ontario, where they appeared to remain till they were grown. They increased in size year by year and were caught frequently in nets near the mouth of the Genesee. Some were large enough to be marketed, and it is possible that they bred of themselves, as their numbers instead of diminishing, augmented. In four years after they were introduced, they were observed in immense shoals at the lower end of the lake. Still it must be borne in mind that both of these fish could descend to the sea, although the journey would be a long one. Moreover, it has not been shown that the salmon feed in Lake Ontario, but some of the shad that were caught in the lake were full of food.

Another interesting experiment resulted with similar success. At the request of the commissioners of California, some twenty thousand shad fry were sent to that state. They were carried through the vicissitudes of their journey safely but at the cost of much labor and anxiety, and were safely deposited in the Sacramento river. Up to that time, shad were wholly unknown in the Pacific coast, so the experiment was nothing less than to introduce them into a new ocean. Of course the undertaking was most doubtful in its results. There were questions of water, food, temperature and so forth, which no man could answer and which had to be referred solely to the fish themselves. Fortunately they rendered a verdict in favor of the attempt. They adapted themselves promptly to their new home; they explored the neighborhood, discovered satisfactory food, made themselves contented and proceeded to possess the land, or rather water. In 1874, shad weighing three and a half pounds, were caught in the Sacramento, which they were ascending evidently for the purpose of spawning, and in 1878, they were an article of commerce and sale in the public markets. It is therefore, possible that within a few years the rivers of the Pacific slope will teem with this excellent fish as abundantly as was once the case with the rivers of the Atlantic states.

Attempts have been made to transport shad eggs and fry in salt water, but without success. The young are delicate at best, and have to be watched with the greatest care during removal from place to place, and the oftener the water can be changed the better; about 6,000 is as many as can be trusted in one milk can, unless for very short journeys. A plan has been suggested for hatching shad and other fish in still water, where there is any power by steam or otherwise, of keeping the boxes in motion. These are made of metal, and are dipped up and down by being hung on the end of a bar lifted and lowered by machinery or otherwise. The point is to keep up a circulation of the current of water, and any arrangement that effects this will hatch the fish.

The time of shad spawning depends upon the temperature of the water of the rivers, which must be between 65° and 80°. This differs on different rivers. On the St. John, in Florida, and in the Savannah River. it is in February; in March shad begin to run into the Potomac, and in May and June they are spawning; in the Hudson the season is still later, usually commencing in May and closing about the 1st of July; in June it begins in the Connecticut, and extends up to the middle of July; so that the farther you go north the later the season is.

It is propable that the introduction of shad even into the tributaries of the Mississippi may be a success. There was a four pound shad taken in the Ohio at Louisville, in 1877, from those that were deposited in 1872, and there were forty or fifty shad taken daily during the entire spring of that year. Reports have come in from many parts of the west giving more or less credible accounts of the capture of shad, although many of the circumstances that there surround them are adverse to their life and growth.

ALEWIVES AND SALT WATER HERRING.—These are to be hatched like shad, and ascend the rivers to spawn at about the same times. Bartram in his "Harvest of the

Sea," p. 168, assures us that in England, the herring spawns and breeds in salt water, and twice in the year. This is not the case in America. We are supposed to have a herring that belongs entirely to the fresh water, but the identity of which is not quite established, but our common herring is migratory in its character, like the shad. Since the shad was introduced into the rivers emptying into Lake Ontario, the herring seems to have appeared there having been seen quite frequently in the spring of 1878 along the shores of the lake and in the streams flowing into it, having entered them apparently for the purpose of spawning.

CHAPTER XIII.

BLACK BASS AND OTHER FISH.

We now come to the consideration of other species of fish that need entirely different treatment. Most of them are rarely cultivated on the purely artificial plan in consequence of peculiarities of their habits or of their *ova*. The fish of which we have already treated have eggs that are loose in the uterine sacs when ripe, and are comparatively free from mucous when emitted. The eggs of the trout adhere at first to whatever they touch, and those of the whitefish need a little agitation for a time; but these qualities do not interfere with their management in troughs or on screens. On the other hand the black bass, the carp and their cognate varieties have eggs that are either surrounded with a glutinous fluid or attach themselves at once and permanently to whatever they touch. Some of them can be rendered free by agitation of the water, which is readily effected by placing the open hand upon it with the fingers distended and moving it up and down. This keeps the eggs in motion while it does not bruise or crush them.

The species of which we shall now treat include the black bass, Oswego bass, strawberry bass, rock bass, white bass, pike perch, striped bass, yellow perch, pickerel, muscalonge, carp, catfish and goldfish. The eggs of the white perch, pike perch, carp and goldfish stick fast to whatever they touch on emission, and must be kept in motion for an hour to remove this tendency. Those of the fresh water bass, yellow perch, pickerel and muscallonge are surrounded with a glutinous matter coming out like long semi-transparent ribbons which may be attached from point to point like a spider's web A change of water is needed for these, but not so strong a current as for the eggs of trout and salmon. The eggs of the striped bass are free from the sticky or glutinous matter, but are about as adhesive as whitefish eggs and need agitation for nearly an hour.

THE BLACK BASS.—This is among the finest sporting as well as food fish in America. It abounds in the clear waters of the Western and Northern lakes; bites fiercely at fly or trowlling spoon, makes a vigorous fight for life, liberty and happiness, showing a perfect willingness " to fight it out on that line if it takes all summer," and at last when subdued and brought to the table does honor to the cook who prepares it, and pleasure to the palate that enjoys it. It is unknown in European countries, and exists solely with us, where its vigor, enterprise, restlessness, and independence, its athletic but not altogether comely appearance make it rather representative in its character. It is self-reliant, and when placed in new waters not merely makes itself at home, but appropriates the locality, explores its furthest recesses and devours its aboriginal inhabitants. It natural distribution was through a few of the lakes of New York, but mainly in the North-western States. It has, however, been acclimated in many other ponds and lakes where it now flourishes extensively. The black bass loves bright, pure, lively water, not as cold as the trout streams of our spring-producing hills and mountains, but free from foul matters held suspended in it, and with motion either of current or from the winds. It deposits its eggs on rocky or pebbly ledges. The parents guard and protect their nests till the young are hatched, and even watch over the latter till they can take care of themselves. Alternately the male and female stands guard over their precious possession of infantile possibilities; if one is away scouring the country for food, the other is on the watch, fierce, brave, resolute, and woe to the unhappy intruder who would steal a dinner from the deposit of bass eggs. The bass is the tyrant of the fresh waters; even the big-jawed, snake-like pickerel cannot stand against him. His teeth are long and sharp, his mouth is large and threatening, his body is close knit and stout, and his fins are arrowed at every point with sharp and poisonous spines. Such a creature mounting guard over his young is not an enemy to be despised. The young need a mother's care for some days after they are hatched. They have scarcely any sac and need food. They cluster around the mother, and she takes them where the food is and teaches them how to get it, until they learn how to provide for themselves—just as an old bird teaches her young, after leaving the nest, how to get their own food—then she leaves them to take care of themselves. It would be just as impossible for a young fish, belonging to the black bass family, to take care of itself just after it was hatched, as it would be for a bird just hatched to take care of itself.

Black bass is one of the most prolific varieties of our fresh water fish. Their natural increase is so great and their growth so rapid that it never has been an object to fish culturists to attempt their artificial propagation. When the spawning season draws near, they select, guided by natural instinct, with great care for the purpose of propagation certain portions of the river having a pebbly or gravelly bottom. From these they remove carefully, all sediment, weeds and sticks. This work completed leaves a clear bright space in the bottom of the river, circular in form, and having a diameter of about three feet. These beds are readily distinguished by the casual observer from the ordinary bottom of the river by their brightness, the gravel having the appearance of being washed or scoured. When the parent fish are ready to spawn the female goes upon this prepared bed and deposits her spawn in a glutinous band or ribbon running in various directions across the bed. She is followed by the male who impregnates the eggs by the expression of his milt.

Their care of the young, (the exercise of which is peculiar to the bass, sunfish and catfish) taken in connection with the fact that a large pair of bass will deposit 20,000 eggs, will give some idea of their fertility. Possibly the fish are capable of reproduction when two years old, having at that time attained the extraordinary length of eight or nine inches, but this is mere conjecture, based more particularly upon our knowledge of the size and weight of the fish at that age. They frequently attain the weight of five and six pounds; in rare instances seven and eight. They are unsurpassed in flavor by any of the perch family.

Some ponds have been stocked with the fry, but it remains to be seen whether this will prove successful.

The fry are very small, and remain but a few days over the beds where they are hatched, so that it requires very close watching to capture them. They are removed just at the time when they are accustomed to have the protection of the parent fish and they are all liable to perish in new water among other species of fish. The common and the most reliable method of introducing the bass is to transport adult fish from well-stocked ponds to new localities. This, when properly done and the water is suitable, has never been known to fail. The fish do not bite freely until after the spawning is over in June, and they do not usually reach their new home until July or later, so that there is no fry from them until the second year. The fish generally selected for transfer are from one to three years old, measuring from three to twelve inches in length. Fish of this size are not only more numerous, but they bear transportation better, and are more readily acclimated than when larger. They are moved with a great deal of difficulty in hot weather, especially when the journey requires more than twelve or fifteen hours; but with care and skill no serious loss need take place. It has been our practice to distribute these varieties during the spring because we had facilities for obtaining full grown fish at that season, but in most localities it would probably be necessary to transport them in summer.

From our present knowledge we cannot recommend hatching black bass by artificial methods, although the eggs if kept in motion at first, can afterwards be developed in the shad hatching boxes or in Holton's boxes. They take five to ten days to hatch. The fish begin spawning in May and complete the operation in June and remain with their young for about fifteen days thereafter.

OSWEGO BASS, WHITE PERCH, ROCK BASS.—The same observations apply to these varieties as to the black bass. They spawn a little earlier, say in May and early June, and are to be treated in the same way. The Oswego bass is not so exacting, however, in the quality of water that it affects as the black bass, it will live in sluggish, warm, discolored streams and ponds where the muddy bottom produces lilies, grasses and weeds. No matter how much earthy matter may at times become suspended in the water, the oswego bass will thrive and be contented. It is known as the "chub" in Virginia and other of the southern states, and is well adapted to most of the ponds of that section of our country. Its flesh is good, although coarser than that of the black bass, and it is the fish for home consumption, and for introduction into by far the larger part of our land where nothing more is demanded than a certain amount of fish food for the table. It is voracious and bites freely at bait or trolling spoon, but does not give the angler much sport, as its resistance is feeble and not sustained. It is mainly distinguished by having a larger mouth than the true black bass, and by having a dusky stripe along the side called the lateral line, which is more visible than in the black bass. They are often confused, and even the scientific names have been muddled and confounded. They were known as *grystes nigricans* for the black bass, and *grystes salmoides* for the Oswego bass, until new appellations were lately applied of *micropterus salmoides* for the small mouthed and *micropterus pallidus* for the large mouthed bass.

PIKE-PERCH.—This fish which passes under many aliases as the grass pike, the pike of the lakes, the wall-eyed pike and pickerel of Canada, is an inhabitant of many of the larger waters of our country, and was formerly abundant. It is also known in localities as the Susquehanna and Ohio salmon. There are several species, which at one time were the subjects of a large and valuable trade, and which are still highly prized for their table qualities. Their numbers have, however, greatly diminished. They require a free range of water, and cannot be confined to the narrow limits of private preserves. Their cultivation and extension are solely a matter of general public interest. They spawn early in April, and the eggs if extruded by hand, must be kept in constant motion for an hour and a half. They may be hatched in the shad and Holton boxes, and require thirty one days for development in water at a temperature of 34°. In warmer water they will mature in ten days.

GOLD FISH AND CARP—May be hatched precisely like pike perch. They spawn in June and can be raised to advantage by the artificial method, as in their natural state the old ones devour the young as fast as they appear. Persons owning gold fish ponds are often surprised that the number of the fish never increases, and explain the phenomenon by the supposition that they do not breed in confinement. This is a mistake; they breed freely and abundantly, but the fry are devoured unless the pond has a shallow shelving edge, with grass or weeds where they can lie and hide from the larger ones. The motion of swallowing is peculiar. The prey is not seized by being darted upon, but is sucked in by a motion of the water into the mouth and out at the gills of the larger fish. The latter will remain motionless while his destined food approaches and pauses before his jaws, when suddenly the youngling is drawn sideways and disappears. The operation is well adapted to the lazy motions of the gold fish.

The eggs of these and kindred varieties may be hatched on baskets made of wicker or boughs, into which they are stripped directly, male and female together. The eggs catch on the twigs and remain there while the basket is deposited in some stream with a gentle current. Or the eggs may be caught on glass and, after being fertilized with the milt, left where the water can flow over them, care must be taken to shake and move the glass so that it is not covered with more than a single layer of eggs. The king carp is strongly recommended for introduction from Europe, where it attains great size and enjoys a high reputation for flavor and succulence. It is distinguished from other and inferior varieties by having only a few scales. There is also an American carp which attains a weight of eight or ten pounds and is occasionally seen in market.

STURGEON.—As an article of food the flesh of this fish is not to be despised. In England, being a royal dish, it is held in high estimation, and every sturgeon captured in the British Isles is the property of Her Majesty.

Experiments were first made in this country in 1874 by the New York Commission to hatch out the eggs of this fish, but, owing to the difficulties experienced in obtaining ripe males and females at the same time, the attempt proved unsuccessful. The year following these difficulties were overcome, and a complete success achieved.

The fishermen were constantly netting sturgeon at New Hamburg, on the Hudson, at the mouth of Wappinger's creek, at which place there appeared to be a natural spawning ground, and on June 7th, at 10, a. m., a ripe male and female were caught. As the fish could not be handled in the ordinary way, the female had to be cut open, after it had been previously ascertained by experiment that the eggs seemed to be perfectly ripe.

The eggs were quickly placed in the pans, and the milt bag cut bodily from the male fish, and the milt pressed out over the eggs.

The eggs were found to come from the fish in an agglutinated sticky mass, somewhat similar to the eggs of the perch or the frog. In order to hatch in the shad boxes, it was necessary that the eggs should be free and not stick together. This is avoided in the case of sticking eggs, by stirring them until the gummy envelope dissolves, or is washed away. It was found almost impossible to do this in the case of sturgeon eggs, but by constant stirring, the eggs appeared at last (thirty minutes to two hours) to be in a state which would justify a trial in the shad boxes. The eggs are larger than those of the white fish and measure about seven to the inch. They are of a dark brownish color, with the yolk showing black through the opaque brown. On June ninth, a brown line showed itself around the eggs, being the first visible formation of the fish. At 3 p. m. on that day, about fifty-three hours after impregnation, the first movement was observed in the fish. Almost all fish embryos move the tail, the head being quiet, these sturgeon seemed to move only the middle part of their bodies, the head and tip of the tail being quiet. On June tenth, at 6 p. m., the young sturgeon commenced to hatch, the next morning by 5 a. m. they were all found hatched out. When turned loose into the river the young fish sought the bottom immediately, hiding in the mud and among the stones. A few of the young were kept until they were an inch long, and could be seen to pick up food from the sides of the box, but it is improbable that they could be kept in confinement by artificial feeding. The food sac was very small and apparently lasted about six days. The time of hatching was about one hundred hours, with the water ranging from sixty-seven to seventy-four degrees.

The importance of the sturgeon as an article of food has never been fully appreciated. They contain, when ripe, enormous quantities of eggs; from fifty to sixty pounds being taken from a full grown fish. From its roe, caviare, the national dish of Russia, is prepared, and a company is now profitably engaged on the Hudson and the upper lakes in its manufacture, and the mature fish attains the enormous size of three hundred pounds. The flesh is yellow and rich, and so nearly does it resemble meat that it has been nicknamed "Albany beef." It is probably possessed of greater muscle giving and hunger appeasing qualities than that of any other fish, the salmon not excepted. It is delicious food when properly prepared. but having in former times been exceedingly cheap, it came to be despised as the food of the poor. Unless something is done for its cultivation it will soon become a delicacy only of the rich.

STRIPED BASS, ROCKFISH OF THE SOUTH.—Contrary to the opinions of most fish culturists, the ova of the striped bass have been found to be entirely free from the gelatinous covering which always surrounds the eggs of the perch, pike, black bass, Oswego bass, etc., etc. It flows from the fish readily, is easily hatched, and the young fish quickly develop.

Fully half a million eggs have been found in females of fair size. Striped bass are more numerous than any other salt water fish of our coast, and yet they are daily growing scarcer. Their habits are little understood, and their times and places of spawning still uncertain. It has been supposed that they spawned at different seasons of the year, and while some investigators were positive that this act was accomplished in fresh water, others were equally confident that it occurred at sea. The most experienced fishermen of the seacoast—men who have followed the business all their lives—have been consulted, but were far from agreeing in their views.

It was certain that a number of these fish were migratory, or at least semi-migratory in their character, visiting the fresh waters at certain seasons, but remaining in the new element for an unknown period. This is proved by their ascending the falls of the Potomac at certain months every year, and their appearing in other rivers at established periods. The supposition was natural that they made this change for the purposes of spawning, and yet it was equally clear that the vast majority of striped bass never left the ocean or the salt bays, coves and lagoons which are connected with it.

Striped bass are the most numerous of the salt water fish of our coast from Maine to Florida. They are with us, more or less, at all seasons of the year. They are the principal means of supplying our markets. They grow to a large size, and are extremely prolific. If they can be cultivated artificially, an immense benefit will be conferred on the community. The only doubt is whether a sufficient number of the spawning fish can be obtained in ripe condition.

Those that spawn in the fresh water ascend the rivers for the purpose in spring, and begin the operation about the month of May. The eggs are expressed without difficulty, and hatch in eight days in the ordinary shad hatching boxes. The fry have little umbilical sac, and may be turned loose immediately, and will take care of themselves. The eggs are about the size of those of the shad.

Striped bass have a peculiar aptitude for both fresh and salt water, and may be changed from one to the other without preparation, and without detriment. They will live and grow if retained in fresh water ponds, to which they may be transported as soon as they are caught in the salt inlets and creeks in which the young usually make their appearance. Whether they will spawn if kept wholly in small preserves, we do not know.

One of the most remarkable experiments in fish culture was made by the New York Commission in the years 1876 and 1877, on the Hudson river. Shad and striped bass were not only successfully crossed, but the young of the mixed breed were hatched in large numbers. The eggs of the shad were impregnated with the milt of the striped bass. Every care was taken to make the experiment conclusive. As male shad were being stripped at the same time, and it was possible that the sperms might be in the water around the boat where the nets were landed and the operations conducted, and consequently impregnation be effected by the milt of the shad itself in that way, the utmost precautions were used to obtain water a safe distance from the boat, and always up against the current. It was thus made certain that the impregnation was effected solely by the milt of the striped bass. The eggs were then deposited in the shad boxes as the bass eggs had been previously hatched, and a very fair percentage of them matured in the ordinary time. There was a marked difference in the appearance of the fry—a difference clearly observable to the practiced eye, but not capable of description on paper.

These results seem almost incredible, and open an entirely new field in fish culture.

If two such wholly dissimilar fish as the striped bass and shad can be crossed, it may be expected that all varieties which spawn at about the same time, and hatch under analogous circumstances, can be treated in the same way. New and remarkable species may even be originated, and as great changes effected as from the crossing of flowers and fruits. This operation was repeated in 1877, and fully ten thousand of this strange combination were hatched and turned free in the river. They must soon prove their capacity for existence, and more or less of them should be caught in 1879 or 1880, enough to call attention to them if they shall have successfully solved the problem of life, and combatted the dangers that encompass them. The adaptability of bass to unusual circumstances, their capacity of living in fresh or salt water, or changing from one to the other, and their independent habits of life, make a favorable result extremely probable. It will certainly be a "queer fish" that shall be compounded of half bass, half shad, and we look to its appearance with interest.

CATFISH.—These have habits somewhat like the black bass. They make nests and guard over them and their young. They spawn in June, and are exceedingly prolific. The young grow rapidly, and should be transported about the time the mother leaves them, while they are still in schools. As food, there are few better fish to eat than the blue catfish, while the yellow variety, though not quite so dainty, is equally satisfying to the cravings of hungry nature. They dig out a room two feet across in the solid mud at the bottom or sides in the stream or pond, and deposit their eggs in that, and lay over them and fan them with their fins until they hatch, which takes place in eight or ten days. They leave a hole open as a sort of door to their hatching chambers to give them egress and ingress.

LOBSTERS.—The American lobster is found upon the Atlantic coast from New Jersey to Labrador, and yet almost nothing has been published in regard to its traits and local distribution. It lives upon rocky, gravelly, and sandy bottom, from low water down to twenty or thirty fathoms and perhaps deeper, but not probably at great depths. It feeds upon any kind of animal matter either fresh or decaying, which it can discover.

In Long Island Sound the lobster fishing begins late in March or early in April, and continues till late in the fall, although the greater part are taken in May and June. On the coast of northern Massachusetts and Maine, whence the winter supply comes, they may be taken nearly all the year round. The time at which the females carry eggs varies very much on different parts of the coast, being later and later as we go further north; south of Cape Cod, in Long Island and Vineyard Sounds, they are found carrying eggs from the first of April till late in June. At Portland, Maine, they were carrying eggs till the middle of August, while in the Bay of Fundy they are found with eggs from mid-summer till September.

Soon after the hatching, the young leave their parent and live for a considerable period a very different life from the adult. At first they are not more than a third of an inch long, and have scarcely any resemblance to a lobster. They are furnished with long swimming branches to the legs and swim about freely in the water, living most of the time near the surface, like many kinds of free swimming shrimps. With each change of the skin they become more and more lobster like, until when a little more than half an inch long they appear like veritable little lobsters, but still have the free swimming habits of the earlier stages. During this period, which must be several weeks, they are constantly exposed to the attacks of fishes and all sorts of marine animals, while they themselves pursue and feed upon still smaller fry. Any attempt to rear great numbers through these stages in confined areas would probably prove unsuccessful, as the young at this time require a great amount of pure sea water and peculiar food, found only where minute, free-swimming animals congregate.

After they become a few inches long, the growth of lobsters is slow. They increase in size only at the times of shedding the shell, which probably takes place only once a year for those of ordinary size, and the increase at each of these changes is moderate, as may be seen by comparing the size of the cast shell with the lobster a few days after leaving it, although the increase of weight is considerable. In lobsters of very large size the shell is not always changed, even as often as once a year.

How early they begin to breed is somewhat uncertain. Females not more than half a pound in weight are, however, found carrying eggs, but in these small females the eggs are comparatively few in number. The average weight of lobsters sold in New York market is about two pounds.

The lobster can be propagated easily, yet there are always more or less difficulties to overcome. One of the principal is to find a place suitable to build a pond, and then to build it so that the young cannot get away. The pond should be built in some place where the salt water sets in from the ocean, and should be screened in such a way that the water can flow in and out with the rise and fall of the tide. It should be fenced on the seaward side, and possibly all around, so as to prevent the lobster from going over the land to the ocean. In June, put in a few thousand lobsters, and we have no doubt there will be a most abundant return. Lobsters carry their spawn under their tails until they hatch, and the young are carried in that way for many days, when they drop off. Thence forward they look out for their own food. A single lobster will hatch as many as 1,000 young. If there are many lobsters in a pond it will be necessary to feed them, but any refuse from a slaughter-house or fish-market will answer for this purpose.

FROG CULTURE.—There are many stagnant pools about the country useless in their present state, which can be utilized by converting them into frog ponds, and the man who could raise a million of frogs and get them safely to market would be a wealthy man. The difficulties to be encountered are many and varied, but can be overcome by patience and perseverance. To those who feel disposed to take advantage of it, the following *results* of two year's experience will prove beneficial.

Take a dipper and go to the pond where the frog casts its spawn. A close examination will reveal a small glutinous mass which is to be dipped up very carefully lest the mass be broken and the spawn lost. Place them in a pail filled with water and take them to your hatching-box, which is made after the fashion of the shad hatching box, two feet long and eighteen inches wide, with No. 12 gas-tarred wire sieving on the bottom. Anchor the box in a gentle current. They will hatch in from seven to fifteen days, according to the temperature of the water. Soon after they are hatched they should be turned loose in a pond prepared with great care, as they have numerous enemies, such as fish, snakes, birds, lizards, coons and many other animals. The pond should be made where the ground is springy, and should have plenty of soft muck at the bottom. In this the frog lies during the winter. The pond should have a light board fence around it so that animals could not get in, and should be built so close to the water that no bird could stand on the inside and pick up the polywogs. It is absolutely necessary to the preservation of the young fry that these precautions should be most strictly adhered to. You will have no trouble in feeding the young while they are polywogs, as nature has provided for that. In all waters they live on what is called sediment that collects on everything lying in the water, unless it is strong impregnated with some mineral.

Examine this sediment under a strong magnifying glass and you will see that it is all animal matter, or a formation between animal and vegetable, and is proper food for the young fry. They will eat it off from the sticks and stones on the bottom of the pond, and keep them perfectly clean. An old pond is better than a new one, as it has more food.

The polywogs will grow and after a while develop into frogs. We cannot give the precise time required for this change as we have had them change in one season or go years without doing so. Probably this depends upon the temperature of the water, and that the warmer it is the faster development occurs. The hind legs break through the skin first and are followed by the front, the perfect frog varying in size according to the size of the tadpole. When it is finally developed the frog requires different kind of food, such as insects, small fish or meat. Naturally it will only take living food, and difficulty may be experienced in teaching it to live on any other. It will eat minnows, young tadpoles, or flies of any kind, but the ooze on which it existed in its transitory state is no longer sufficient. Flies may be attracted to the pond by placing stale meat around it, and minnows can be supplied in certain quantities but the question of feeding the frog is the difficulty in frog culture.

There are several varieties of these batrachians, some of the southern sorts will weigh over a pound apiece. The largest edible sorts should be selected and the market for them will be found to be unlimited at a price hardly surpassed by that paid for fresh trout.

Great care should be taken in gathering spawn, not to get toad spawn. Frog spawn is laid in a bunch like a bunch or sponge of jelly. It is clear with black spots in it, but turns white when dead. It should be gathered carefully and the jelly which is essential to successful hatching, should be broken as little as possible. Toad spawn is laid in a string, the female, when laying her eggs, walks back and forth carrying on her back the male, who is impregnating the eggs with melt as they are emitted. When lying in the water, it looks like glass tubes with No. 4 shot destributed the fourth of an inch apart the entire length of the tubes. Frogs attain their growth in from three to five years. We have recommended putting the spawn in a hatching box, but the eggs will hatch as well in the pond without a box, if they are not liable to depredation by enemies. And if the meat that is put around the pond to attract flies, is cut up finely, the frogs will soon get a taste of it and learn to eat it. When they have passed beyond the pollywog into the frog state, they must have a chance to get out of the water among the grass, and if the pond is near the house, (as it should be,) there is less danger from animals. We have seen taken from a spring hole in winter, a solid mass of frogs as large as a bushel basket.

PRESERVING FLUID.—The ordinary methods of preserving specimens of eggs and fish, have never proved satisfactory. We have obtained the following receipt, and have tested it thoroughly, both for delicate young fry and for fish eggs, and have found it entirely successful, and far superior to the preparations usually employed. It preserves the natural colors in almost their full brilliancy, whereas spirits of any kind destroy them, and both the fish and the eggs are as nearly like what they appear in the water, as it is possible to conceive. For microscopic observations, it is invaluable as it is perfectly transparent and presents the growth of fungus absolutely. Eggs that have been kept in it for weeks, retain every appearance of life, they exhibit the various stages of embryonic development precisely as if they were just taken from the trough, the changed colors of the living or dead eggs are preserved and the outlines of the embryo, its eyes, its membranes and bones are plainly visible. It is said to preserve specimens uninjured for years, but certainly our experience justifies us in strongly recommending it to all who desire to preserve specimens temporarily or for merely microscopic and scientific investigation, while we have no reason to doubt that it would answer equally well for a longer time. The objections to any other preparations, are numerous, as every one who has tried them is aware, but this appears to meet every difficulty and can be safely used by any one. In preserving the delicate and evanescent colors of fish, it adds immensely to the value of the specimens, which in the ordinary preserving fluid, were of a dull unattractive and unnatural sameness of hue, that not only destroyed their beauty but rendered them almost undistinguishable. We give the letter as we receive it.

ROCHESTER, N. Y.

The preservative Fluid, which we prepared for you, for the preservation of the *ova* of fishes, is composed of equal parts of Glycerine and Camphor Water. The Glycerine should be the best quality—(Price's English or Bower's American.) This fluid is very highly recommended by Lionel S. Beale, F. R. S. Mr. Beale has preparations which have been preserved in Glycerine for twenty years. The addition of Camphor Water prevents any tendency to mildew. Another advantage, and one of especial value in the preservation of *ova* in the Glycerine and Camphor Water fluid, is, that specimens can be prepared and forwarded during cold weather without danger of loss by freezing.   Respectfully yours,

C. F. PAINE & CO.

CHAPTER XIV.

FISH CATCHING.

We now come to the second division of our work. Having told our readers how to hatch fish, we will now tell them how to catch them. We do not propose to enter into a minute consideration of the subject, but shall confine ourselves to a few general directions. Greater detail would make this book too large, elaborate and expensive; but there are suggestions and advice which will be found of value to fishermen, who may then supplement this information by experience recorded in a more elaborate form in other works. There are many ways of taking different fish; some of them are good, some bad, and some indifferent. We shall only give the best, and mention those points which are often neglected, or not observed, and which are essential to what has come to be designated as "good luck." There is more skill than luck in fishing, as in most things; and the man who possesses the most skill will, in the long run, enjoy the most luck.

There are two peculiarities of all sorts of fish, which are frequently unnoticed; that they are largely attracted to their food by scent, and that they feed at night. In all muddy streams it is only by scent that they can discover their food, for their eyes are no more capable of piercing a turbid and discolored medium than ours. At such times which are the best for the purpose, as the flood, which causes the roiliness of the water, carries down worms, grubs, and other food, it is apparent that they must rely wholly upon the acuteness of their powers of smell. On such occasions it is wholly useless to use artificial baits of any kind that only appeal to the sight, and flies, trolling spoons, or artificial minnows, are out of place.

Then, again, when fish are scattered, and are to be attracted to a special spot, recourse must be had to similar means. It is a well known plan in striped bass fishing to use chopped menhaden to cause a "slick" or floating streak of oil that will be carried long distances by the tide or waves. The same thing is done with still fishing for blue-fish, and without this assistance but few of either of these varieties would be taken on the sea coast. The same idea may be utilized in other ways, and prove how fish may be allured to their destruction by their noses as well as their palates.

It is possible that strong smelling substances can be employed advantageously on baits. This has been maintained by many writers on angling. Assafœtida has been recommended among other things for the purpose, but we cannot say what its value is, having never tried it. The main point to be borne in mind is, that in endeavoring to catch fish as much attention must be paid to the scent as to the sight. They must be hungry indeed, or of the coarsest varieties, if they will take stale, rotten and offensive bait, and it is not to be supposed that because our noses are not available under water, theirs are not. The fresher the bait the better it is, as many a bass fisherman has found out in a blind sort of way with his shedder crab or his bony-fish, which are successful when firm and fresh, but are ignored when old and unpalatable. It is said that eels will eat putrid meat, but even this we deny, at least so far as to say that they will seek it when in good order much more ardently.

There are several blind fish in the State preserves, some of which have lived in confinement for years. They have to contend for their share of the daily food against their fellows who are in possession of all their faculties. Nevertheless they manage to get their full rations, and keep as fat as the fattest. The food is thrown in at intervals, and the fish being hungry, and knowing from habit what it is, dart at it without fear, making the water boil and foam. It would seem as though only the most active could obtain any, and in the struggle pieces of meat which are too large to be swallowed at once, are often torn from mouth to mouth. Amid this hurly-burly and confusion, the blind would seem to stand a poor chance; and yet against such odds they hold their own. Their powers of scent must be wonderfully developed, for it is on them alone they can rely. They do not go grubbing on the bottom for such pieces as may have escaped attention, and have sunk, but they dart into the crowd of ravenous creatures, and carry off their proportion in fair fight. Compared with man's helplessness when deprived of sight, their self reliance is incredible, and must be seen to be fully believed.

There are rivers and lakes which are always turbid, and in which all piscatory life would cease were dependence for food to be placed alone on sight. The Mississippi is an example, its waters are never clear, but carry an amount of sediment which must render vision at more than a short distance impossible. It is not suited to a great variety of fish, but such as dwell in it are fat, and often attain great size. In the rivers and waters of the

Mammoth Cave, the fish are wholly eyeless, and yet they manage to obtain food without difficulty. Such instances and evidences prove conclusively that the sense of smell must be consulted in angling nearly as carefully as the sense of sight, and that stinking bait will not answer for a "lucky fisherman."

Another way of taking advantage of the sense of smell in fish is to fill a box perforated with small holes with bait and sink it at night or in roily water, so as to attract the fish. The best attainable food should be used, such as worms or what is even preferable, the spawn of other fish. The scent passes out through the holes and the game is drawn together and made more eager by the appetizing smell and the impossibility of getting at the food. The fisherman then offers them his bait with a hook and line included and they cannot refuse him, but are quickly deluded into his basket. This is somewhat of a poaching and unfair method of fishing, but it is successful.

But not only do fish possess in a high degree the sense of smell, but they are possessed of a smell of their own. We do not mean that "ancient and fish like smell" which comes to all fish equally, the bony fish and the salmon alike, when they have been left out of water for a length of time but a delicate and perceptible odor that clearly distinguishes one species from another so positively that a person who has studied it can tell them apart blindfold. A little investigation will satisfy any one with keen olfactory organs of this fact, and that each kind of fish gives out a peculiar characteristic perfume that can be recognized with a reasonable amount of practice. The odor of the smelt is plainly perceptible, it is supposed to have given the name to the fish, and is observed to differ in the two common varieties of smelt, being much stronger in one than in the other. This is by no means the only instance: some species are easily distinguishable, while with others more experience is required.

It is too much the habit with all anglers to seek their sport only during the day, for often better fishing and far pleasanter can be had at night. So common is this mistake, that few persons know that fish, as a general thing feed more freely at night than during the sunlight hours. In some trout streams the largest trout are never taken during the day. Caledonia brook is an instance. In its waters which are as clear as liquid glass, the big fellows, the wise, cunning grandfathers who have seen such deceptive offerings as flies before, cannot be tempted from their safe retreats under logs and stones so long as daylight lasts during the months of July and August. Only when the sun has disappeared and darkness rules can the fisherman hope to lure them to his creel with some large, light colored fly; then no moon must interfere with her "ray serene," but the darker the time the more suitable it is. A little piece of worm on the point of the hooks adds to its killing qualities on such occasions.

In other matters such as bass fishing, we have thought the moon to be an advantage. If it does not guide the prey to the lure it at least lends beauty to the scene and bathes in its pale light the surroundings of the fisherman, which are often so exceedingly beautiful. In addition, it assists him in his work and enables him to handle his tackle more easily and play his fish more comfortably.

It is not in every locality, nor with all varieties of fish that night fishing is successful. In the ponds of Long Island, although trout are often caught by poachers on set lines, they are rarely taken with the fly at night, and fishing for them would not pay for the trouble. Whether fish will bite or rise at night is a question that must be determined in different localities by trial. We do not know any rules or principles that govern. There are only few kinds of fish that we know of that always, in all places and on all occasions bite better at night than during the day, and those are our uneasy friends, the eel, and bullhead and catfish. Darkness suits their sinuous nature.

The next suggestion of general application is the desirability of using the finest tackle that can be obtained and that is otherwise suitable. When we look at the heavy rods, the clumsy materials, the coarse lines and the huge flies that are so much in vogue, we wonder that any fish are caught, and feel that we cannot too often or too earnestly press upon those of our readers who desire to reach more than mediocrity in the art the necessity of fine tackle. We have found anglers fishing for salmon with a three-ply twisted leader fit to haul over the rocks the heaviest bass, and almost capable of defying the shark-like jaws of the blue fish. We have seen gentlemen at the club houses along the coast where they would be expected to be educated and refined, using double brass wire for leaders, to catch striped bass in the surf in order to escape the occasional raids of the blue fish. But more objectional than all, the practice of a large part of our trout fly-fishermen is to use a leader of gut heavy enough to hold a salmon. Anglers who do these things will never be "lucky." Instead of sighing for better fortune or envying their brethren who bring in better filled baskets they should heed these words, and get better tackle.

It is true that until the angler who has used his coarse tackle gets accustomed to the more delicate, till the fly-fisherman for instance, overcomes the habit of "striking with all his might," advised by one famous writer, he will meet with a "smash up" now and then, and lose some fish. It is also true that in fishing for striped bass in the surf with a single gut, a blue fish will frequently cut the line and carry off bait and hook. But these are matters which can be cured by practice or borne with equanimity, and do not compare with the sense of degradation that one feels when a brother of the angle catches all the fish and carries off all the honors.

If we find that we are taking nothing, while our neighbor is doing well and having fine sport, we should, instead of denouncing the fates, attribute the disparity in nine cases out of ten to his finer tackle, unless we can see that he is a better fisherman than ourselves. We should try to find out at once in what our inferiority lies and remedy it without delay. So accustomed are people to common and rude implements, that they will at first think it impossible to have better. The tautog fisherman as a case in point, has always used a stick, a string and a hook, or what is even inferior, a hand line, and to tell him that he would do better with a short leader of silk-worm gut, would make him stare and laugh, yet the change would often, especially in still, clear water double his catch.

The rule should be an invariable one, that for fish under ten pounds, a leader of gut not heavier than that known as salmon gut should be used. This will bear a direct strain of six pounds, and should enable a skillful angler to kill a salmon that would weigh fifty, if not a hundred. An ordinary flax line will part at about a strain of twenty-five pounds, and a three-ply twisted gut leader will support about eighteen pounds. A fish in the water cannot pull as much as half his dead weight out of it, and under the pliancy of the rod does not exert one fifth as much force; so that even a fine trout leader which will not sustain two pounds, direct pull, will kill a fish of many times that weight, if scientifically managed. In giving these estimates of resistances, we would say they were tested by spring balances to which the lines were tied, and as the rupture always occurred at the knots, it is probable we have somewhat understated the strength of the materials.

It must be understood that in this part of this work we are not writing for mere novices, and we presume that the reader has mastered the rudiments of the anglers art, and has had more or less practice. We put forward such hints and suggestions as our experience has taught us to believe, even good fishermen have not always noticed, and which if acted on, will tend to perfect the performance of those who have passed the stage of mere beginners and desire to hold the rank of adepts. Our directions will not be extended, and will not cover the simplest fishing rules or maxims, but will be confined to what may be regarded rather as finishing touches with reference to whatever is new, and not mentioned by other writers, with perhaps a few other ideas that are peculiarily our own.

CHAPTER XV.

FISHING FOR THE SALMON FAMILY.

Fly Fishing.—Casting the fly is essentially the same sort of art, whether it is cast for salmon or for trout, and is the highest development of the angler's skill. It is no more difficult, perhaps, than casting the bass bait; but the delicacy of rod, line and fly required, place it at the head of all kinds of angling. In salmon fishing a two-handed rod of some twenty ounces weight is used, with one hundred yards of line, a stout single gut leader, and a large fly. In trout fishing a single-handed rod of ten to fourteen ounces, a leader of the most delicate gut ten feet long, and never over eleven, and three small flies, are the proper implements. But the motion and method of casting the fly are in both instances essentially the same; and the man who can wield the pliant trout rod deftly, will in a few hours' practice master the stouter and more powerful salmon rod.

There are all sorts of fly rods manufactured, and each sort has its advocates. There is the stiff elastic rod, made of cedar or bamboo; the double action, made of ironwood and greenheart, and the tough, slow rod, made of ash, spruce, or hickory. The first is suited to the man of quick eye and hand, impatient of the slower motions of the others; the second is adapted to the deliberate fisherman, who goes on the plan that fish hook themselves; and the third is suited to the careless man, who will never acquire the higher development of his art, but wants something strong, that will not smash up on the first pound fish that startles him with its unexpected rise, and which he strikes " with all his might," and endeavors to "yank," without more ado, from its native element. We do not mean in making the above distinctions of material, to say that each kind of rod may not be manufactured out of the wood spoken of, as appropriate to the other; but we only mention the materials as they are usually applied.

We prefer the spongy elastic rod, that sends the fly straight out, even directly against the wind, and which controls the line to the very stretcher fly, under all circumstances, and on all occasions. But to use such an implement requires strength, often the entire muscular power of an unusually strong arm. Where two fishermen are equally skillful, the strongest will invariably cast his fly the farthest. Let there be no mistake about this; in fly fishing there is not merely an application of delicate manipulation, but often the violent exertion of the utmost strength. It is the combination of the two qualities that wins. A line seventy feet in length is heavy, and the wrist and arm must be vigorous that can lift it from the water and send it out extended to its full length behind the fisherman. The difficulty is not so much in the forward delivery of the line as in recovering it, and the man who can clear the line well behind him, can usually send it out over the water with the help of the wind, that must favor him always to enable him to make a very long cast. In casting against the wind, the same strength is necessary, but it is expended on a shorter cast, and in overcoming the opposition of the wind while the line is being delivered.

A limber double action rod casts a line neatly and easily. It is the king of rods for short casts in moderate weather, and with the wind; but for rough work it will not meet the highest demands. The man of moderate muscles and sinews should stick to it, and the lazy mediocre angler will prefer it; but the ambitious sportsman, who wants to be "head of the heap," and do the best that can be done, who must cast over a "break to windward," or reach a promising spot a long way off, or jerk his fly under an overhanging branch if there is a hope that a trout lies *perdu* near the bank on the other side, and who demands a tool that will respond to his efforts, will condemn it as not up to the mark. Mr. Thaddeus Norris made his rods, which were of the double action, with a ridge on each side, so as to give them more stiffness if they were held edge forward, but we were never convinced that this remedied the difficulty.

The great point in selecting a rod is for the angler to adopt the kind that is suited to him; get one that gives play to his best powers, and then stick to it. This is not an easy matter, and our readers will be fortunate if they succeed without many trials and much disappointment. There is always one rod that suits one man, and possibly there may never be another. The endeavor is to bring these together, and once joined they should never be sundered till death doth them part. But it is no easy matter for the fisherman to tell just when he has the rod that fits his body and mind. He gets accustomed to one, and a new one comes "awkward" to him for a time. At present prices they are expensive playthings, and only the richest gentleman can go on testing results at a cost of twenty five to fifty dollars for each experiment. We can only assist in the process by making such suggestions as we have offered above.

In winning matches in fly casting, and in acquiring a great reputation for casting prodigious length of line, the rod is of essential importance. It must be backed by skill and strength; but if it is weak and faulty, its owner will never take first rank. The difference between rods is enormous, and there is not one in a hundred, we might say one in a thousand, that will do its work as that work should be done, no matter how admirably it is handled. The fault does not lie in the material, nor wholly in the taper, but there is a subtle something, like the lines of a fast yacht, which cannot be discovered or described, but which distinguish failure from success. Of all the rods, hundreds in number, that the authors of this book have owned, only one was suited to each, and one of those being lost, has never been replaced.

It is utterly impossible to select a rod in the shop where it is sold. It might as well not be handled at all as handled there. The only test is use on the stream. We do not know whether any of the makers will permit this test, common as it has become with guns, but it should always be demanded. A rod need not be injured or defaced in the least by a day's careful use; and it is as much to the interest of the manufacturer as to that of the fisherman, that the latter should be satisfied. Doubtless the suggestion should be complied with by our dealers as soon as its reasonableness is explained to them. In this way some idea of what is desired can be obtained, but the choice of a good rod is a matter of time or luck.

As to material of which the rod should be made, there is probably no preference among the higher classed woods. Bamboo, if split or inlaid on cedar, is the most expensive, and is now the favorite. Iron wood was the preference of the late Mr. Norris. Greenheart had a great run for a time, and in the hands of a careful man cedar, although brittle, is excellent; but ash will make a fairly good rod, and so will lancewood, although the latter is rather heavy. We speak of the second joints;

the butt may be of anything, and the top should always be of split bamboo. We have a very nice little rod of spruce, which was made as an experiment by a friend, and presented to us. It will not cast far, but for light work it responds neatly and easily. It is doubtful whether the quality of the wood is wholly decisive as to the qualities of the rod, and should only be taken into consideration generally.

It is the fashion now to use trout rods, weighing not more than eight ounces. They are artistic and pretty little implements; and for streams or short casts on ponds, are very pleasant. They will not cast a hundred feet, however; no, nor much more than half that distance. But they do not tire the wrist; and where fish are as scarce as they have become in the more settled regions of our land, they will probably remain in vogue. Where long casts are imperative, and it is important to kill large fish in a reasonable time, they will not answer. They should never be carried to the wilds of Lake Superior, Maine, or Canada, but their use should be restricted to Long Island ponds, or the trout brooks of the Middle and some of the Eastern States. Although we have recommended fine tackle, we do not approve of what is too fine to be effective. The eight ounce rod in its place is very beautiful, but all places do not belong to it. It is far preferable, however, to a fly-rod that weighs a pound or over, and that is suitable to no place, being not heavy enough for salmon, nor light enough for trout. A trout fly-rod for all work should weigh from twelve to fifteen ounces, according to the physical strength of its owner.

Similar observations, varied to suit the varied cases, apply to salmon rods. We never use a salmon fly-rod under eighteen feet in length. On the broad rivers of Canada and the British Provinces, the casts are often long, and sometimes extremely difficult. Frequently there will be a rocky precipice at the angles back, and only a narrow ledge for him to stand on. If, under such disadvantages, he shall find salmon breaking at the further extremity of the pool, which cannot be reached from the other side, he is apt, unless he has a long, powerful rod, to smash many of his hooks, miss many of his fish in consequence, and utter many thoughtless and incomplete observations. Trout can usually be approached, because the streams in which they lie are navigable by boat, or fordable by man; but with salmon this is different, and the fly must be sent where they are, whether at the foot of a fall or the head of a rapid, either of which would soon use up a man, or his frail boat, if exposed to its fury.

A salmon rod of twenty feet is in some waters preferable to one even of eighteen. Weight is not so objectionable in salmon as in trout fishing, for the reason that in the former both hands and arms are used, and there is not such wear and tear of the wrist. A dozen casts will usually determine whether salmon are in the humor for rising in any pool, and then it is as well to wait for a few moments till their humor changes, as to go on urging the fly on their notice. This gives a rest to the fisherman; and as his ground for fishing is always limited, he is not overworked by the handling of his rod. Killing his fish is what tires his muscles. With trout this is different, and the trout fisherman has no rest either while wading a stream for miles at any pool in which he may rise a fish, or while moving from spot to spot in a boat about a pond, where he can only fill his creel by persistent effort.

In our country a salmon stream is ordinarily a mighty river, dangerous, and at places impassable to the frail canoe, which alone can navigate it. It cannot be waded, and the fisherman must be careful not to get within the grasp of its powerful current. It abounds with cataracts, whirlpools, and rocky rapids, in which the canoe is as helpless as the man; but in which the salmon, enjoying the rush and turmoil of waters, love to lie. Perched on some commanding rock, the angler must reach all portions of the stream, and cannot select his station or move from place to place. He must accept the opportunity that nature offers and make the most of it. When he has once been so situated, and found his fifteen foot rod unable to command the best pools or the best parts of them, he will register a solemn oath never again to be caught in such a foolish fix, and he will keep that oath better than he does some others. One lesson will be amply sufficient for his full enlightenment.

LINES.—Practically there is but one line for fly-fishing, either for salmon or trout, the braided silk covered with a water-proof preparation, and tapered. We have a fondness theoretically for the horse-hair line, on account of its lightness, but we never use it now. The superiority of the water-proof line is so marked in every point but lightness, which in itself is a qualified advantage, that no one at present uses any other. It should be tapered at both ends, in order to turn it end for end as it wears out, the first portion to give way being that which is most exposed. These lines were at first only made in England, but now they are being generally manufactured here, of a quality scarcely if at all inferior to the imported article.

The trout line is from twenty to thirty yards long, according to the size of fish it is expected to catch, and the salmon line is one hundred yards in length. The latter is heavier in the center, but they both taper to nearly equal fineness. Weight is necessary to make a long cast, or to cast at all well against the wind; and a splash in the water is avoided by the taper and the casting line. Such a line will last a lifetime with care, and without care will outwear a half-dozen of the best horse hair lines ever made. It never has to be dried, except out of abundant caution in case the entire roll on the reel should get soaked. It is strong and reliable, and has no weak places. It will not cut, and it does not catch in the rings of the rod. Old fishermen who read these words, and who have used hair lines, will appreciate the weight of what we say.

The hair line is lighter, and can be made under certain circumstances, to fall more gently on the water, but in recommending fine tackle we do not mean to recommend any that is too fine to be practical. Some men use a light, limber rod in bass fishing, because, as they say, it takes them longer to kill their fish. This is Miss Nancyism, and there is nothing we despise more. Use the most effective tackle under all circumstances; for coarse fish, strong line and rod; for shy fish fine lines and gut leaders, but always that which will kill the most in the shortest time, and with the greatest ease and certainty. When you go sailing for blue fish it would be a folly to use a line so thin that it would cut your hands and might not hold your fish; but in casting for trout in clear water, you must fish far and fish well, and to do this the water-proof line, all things considered, will be found to be the best.

CASTING LINE.—More important even than the line is the casting line or leader, as we usually call it, made of lengths of silk-worm gut. For the salmon fishing it should be of round, clear, transparent single strands, not too heavy, but tough and strong, and tapered, by choosing the heaviest for the upper portion. No double or twisted leader is ever necessary, for in a steady pull a single strand will break any rod. When the smash up occurs, it usually comes from striking too hard, and may be avoided by leaving the reel free except for the restraint of the click, and not holding the hand on the line. When a salmon is struck he often makes a plunge for the bottom, so that if the angler both holds fast the line and strikes too hard, he will part something—his leader, whether it be single ply or three ply, or in default of that, his rod. Salmon are as shy as trout, and the tackle to deceive them must be as little alarming as possible.

For ordinary trout fishing—we do not refer to Maine or Canada, which exact heavy tackle—the gut lengths can hardly be too fine. They should be tapered the same as the salmon casting line, but should be infinitely more delicate. The gut for the purpose is sometimes drawn down through a guage, but we fancy that taking off the outer skin weakens it, and we prefer to select the finest strands of the roundest and most transparent hanks. You can judge of its excellence by the wiry way in which it resists the teeth when it is bitten. All leaders should be at least two feet shorter than the rod, or otherwise in landing heavy fish, the upper knot will enter the tip ring, and cause much trouble, with possibly the loss of the fish.

We cannot too often repeat, or too strongly impress upon our readers, the necessity for the finest casting lines in fishing in clear, bright waters, where the trout have been taught to be shy, and comprehend the deception that surrounds the "cruel hook." There are moments, rare indeed, happily rare for the continuance of our sport, in which trout lay aside their suspicions, and submit to the most bungling attempts at betrayal; but let no novice put his faith in these. They are of rare occurrence, and short duration; ordinarily the willful creature must be beguiled and tempted in the most subtle manner to be won, and the less visible the "entangling alliances" about the line, the more probable the success. Ninety-nine flies in a hundred, dressed in the shops, are tied on gut nearly twice as stout as it should be; but the dealers, as an excuse, say they cannot sell them otherwise. It is to meet this assertion that we have dwelt so long and earnestly on the advisability of casting fine lines over fine waters. We have hundreds of trout in our ponds that were taken with a fly, and they know the fish rod for years. If you hold a rod over the pond they are out of sight as soon as they can find a place to hide.

FLIES.—This is a subject of infinite variety. We scarcely know where to begin, nor how much to say. We would advise every angler to learn to tie his own flies—not that he will or should always do so, because it would often be an inexcusable waste of time—but in order that he may be able to thoroughly know a good fly when he sees one. The only perfect critic of a picture is a man who can paint, so the only correct judge of a fly is one who has made them. The art of fly tying is by no means difficult; there is not the same labor expended in the operation that there was formerly. The wings are rarely reversed, and good varnish makes up for defects in finish. The best and shortest way to learn the *modus operandi* is by taking lessons from a friend, or a professional. A half dozen lessons, with some practice, will teach all the essentials.

The fly-tyer needs a few utensils—such as spring-pliers, bench vise, mohair, floss silk, gold and silver tinsel, varnish, hooks, sewing silk, and feathers of many kinds, especially the hackles from cocks' necks.. The feathers may be wrapped in paper; even put into open envelopes, if the whole is kept in a box with a few pieces of camphor. No insect is so easily defied as the moth—and none, we believe, does such an enormous amount of damage. There are very few things that a moth can or will eat; but those that he does fancy are often valuable, and them he destroys utterly—furs, flannels, feathers; but above all feathers are his delight. He simply revels in the careless fisherman's stock of flies, or fly-tying materials. Yet he cannot penetrate through a leaf of this book, though he be starving on one side with abundant plenty—a groaning board of delicious feathers of most delicate fibre on the other. He would perish miserably within scent of paradise. Neither can he get through cotton goods of any kind.

How many anglers wail yearly over the destruction of their flies by moths, and it may not be amiss to add here how many anglers' wives compel their husbands to replace ruined furs at more than the cost of a dozen pleasant fishing trips, when the simplest precautions are absolute guaranty of safety. Place books, flies, feathers, furs or flannels, either in paper, gummed with mucilage at the edges, or in bags of muslin or linen, or cotton goods, of any kind, and no evil minded moth can ever enter. If there are no moths or moth eggs in the fabric or materials when put away, none will ever get in. For fly books, the simplest plan is to have a muslin bag a little longer than the book, with a tape sewed fast an inch or two from the mouth. Put the book in, twist round the end of the bag tight, and tie the tape firmly. That is all, and all mothdom will gnash its teeth in helpless rage. Other things may be put in large bags of brown paper, which of course must not have holes in it, and the end can be gummed, or rolled over several times—for moths will follow an opening, however narrow, some distance, if they scent game beyond, and the parcel is then to be tied with a string. The man who does this with the precious means of his sport, can sleep easy, with no nightmares of merciless moths to disturb his mind.

As for the colors of flies, we can only say they should be of all colors. Their hues are infinite, and their name is legion, and forever changing at that. Old and well known varieties are continually coming up under new names, till no man can keep the run of them. What with the alterations of the names of flies, and the improvements in the learned names of fish, it has got to such a pass that the poor angler no longer can honestly tell what he catches, nor what he takes it with. If the fly dealers, on one hand, and the savans of the Smithsonian Institute on the other, keep on, we poor simple-minded fishermen had better give up, or we shall soon know as little what we are talking about as other people.

There are delicate shades and differences of color in flies which affect their killing qualities whatever writers who love to generalize may claim. Every angler has known a half worn out fly at certain times, although its feathers were partly gone and its color almost washed out, prove more taking than a fresh one of precisely the same kind. There are times when trout and salmon will accept simply one fly and no other. These cases are rare, but they will occur. No rule can be given to meet them, and the flies used in different localities are so entirely different that no special directions can be given concerning their selection. Let the angler have a fairly well filled book, and then if he is visiting an untried stream let him consult some one who has fished it before him. The salmon flies for American waters are more simple, less gorgeous in golden pheasant topknot than the English and Scotch, and for sea trout and the trout of Long Island and the ocean coast the red ibis is in vogue, while it is generally discarded on inland waters. The latter peculiarity has been explained on the theory that trout having access to salt water take it for shrimp. There is only one objection to this explanation; shrimp are red, it is true, but only after they have been boiled, and as trout do not boil their shrimp so far as we know, the resemblance to an ibis is lost.

We cannot within the limits of this work give rules relating to the colors and make of the innumerable flies that are used; for that a book equally voluminous would be needed, but there are points in reference to their size which must be borne in mind, and partial directions that we can give for their tying. For large, turbulent, rough waters, and early in the season, large flies are needed, but in bright, summer weather on clear streams or ponds they should be as small as they can be made. There is a regular natural gradation between these points. In Lake Superior, a large, coarse, red hackle made "buzz" as it is called, that is, with the hackle standing out the whole length of the body is probably the most killing. For Caledonia brook and the ponds of Long Island, in the day time during July and August, it is only the smallest midges made of various colors that will take at all. On dark days larger flies may be used than in sunshiny weather.

In disposing the three flies on the leader or casting line, the largest should be used as the upper dropper and the smallest as the stretcher. This arrangement will maintain the taper of the line and make them fall more lightly on the water. The gut lengths that fasten the droppers to the leader should be short, the upper say four inches and the second three, and they should be tied one about a foot or eighteen inches from the end of the main line, and the other half way between that and the stretcher. For very short casts in small brooks more very small fish can be taken in a given time if the three flies are placed only about two feet apart and with long strands to the droppers, so that they may be all trailed along the surface together. This arrangement is to be adopted by enthusiastic anglers who aspire to take a thousand trout averaging an ounce apiece in a summer day, but will not suit fishermen who seek larger fish.

A neat and ingenious invention in fly books has been made by a gentleman in New York, for holding the flies on small hooks like those of the hooks and eyes of ladies' dresses. The plan is not patented and enables the angler to quickly remove or replace one fly without disturbing the others. It may be applied to an ordinary letter envelope of parchment paper which can be made to hold a dozen flies and answer all the purposes of a fly-book, for a day's fishing.

Hooks.—As to the selection of the best shape of hook for fly tying, there is a difference of opinion between the editors of this work, and the reader will have to choose between them. One favors his own discovery and what has come to be called the "needle point hook," because it was originally made from the pointed half of a needle, and the other prefers the sproat. The needle point hook has no barb, being in this particular like the hook of the Chinese, but the point is carried well forward. There is no danger from what most people would suppose might be the objection to it—the loss of fish after they are hooked. It holds precisely as well as if it had a barb, but the point is so long that there is risk—in the opinion of the associated author—of the fish rising short and pulling vigorously at the tail feathers of the suppositious insect without getting his lips over the point. This may only be an objection in certain waters and with shy-rising fish, but it is guarded against by the sproat in which the point of the hook is almost at the very tail of the fly. The approval or disapproval of the needle point or barbless hook will depend probably upon the habits of the trout among which it is used. If they rise well it will be accepted, if they rise short it will be discarded. The want of a barb has one great advantage, the fish can be so readily and quickly taken off the hook. This is sometimes of great importance to the fish breeder who may use a needle point hook in order not to injure the fish he wishes to take and keep for spawners.

FLY TYING AND SALMON FLIES.—It is generally considered that fly making cannot be taught by written instruction, but at all events there is something that the experienced, and an immense deal that the partially instructed beginner may add to his store of knowledge, and if the following directions will not make a novice perfect, they may aid him when he has had a few personal lessons. To tie a fly, the gut should be singed in a candle, or bitten at one end, and the hook and thread waxed to insure the hook's not coming off, which, when a fine fish has it in his mouth, is a heart-rending casualty. Take a few turns with thread on the shank of the bare hook, nearly to the head, then applying to gut, whip it firmly on by working back to the bend; under the last turns at the bend insert whisks for the tail, dubbing, floss or herl for the body, and tinsel if desired. The floss, silk, and dubbings are generally spun or twisted in with the thread, and then wound back toward the shoulder, but they may be wound on before, with or after the thread. Care must be taken that the turns at the bend be firm, and when the material is carried back the body is finished with a couple of turns of the silk, a hackle is then introduced and firmly secured by the smaller end. Wind the hackle around the hook at the place where it is inserted, and when it is sufficiently thick, and the fibres which constitute the legs stand out well, tie it down. Prepare your wings by stripping off the requisite number of fibres from two feathers that are mates so as to have the two wings alike, tie them on and finish off. Securely fasten the thread with half hitches, or by passing the end under several turns, and varnish with a little copal varnish. To make a buzz-fly, that is, one with the hackles the whole length of the body instead of only at the shoulder, insert a hackle at the bend at the same time with the body and tail, and twist it around the body after that is put on, and fasten it at the shoulder. The wings are sometimes laid on pointing up the shank, and afterward bent down and secured in their places. If this is done the head need not be varnished.

To make a salmon-fly, the following additional directions, most of which apply equally to carefully made trout flies, will be found convenient. Tie on the gut as before directed; upon reaching the bend fasten the spring pliers on to the thread, and do not take them off till the fly is finished. Take two turns with the silk over a strip of tinsel, pass the latter several times around the hook to form the tag, fasten it with the silk and cut it off; introduce the floss for the tip, take several turns evenly, tie it down and cut off the end; introduce the tail, and then a piece of herl, wind the herl at the root of the tail and fasten it; take in a new piece of tinsel and a hackle by rubbing back all the fibres but a few at the point, leave both pointing from the head; take a small piece of mohair between your fingers, break it over and over again into small pieces, lengthen it out and twist it round the silk toward the left, as otherwise it will unlay in winding; wind the silk and mohair together round the shank to the shoulder; leave a space of bare hook at the head sufficient for the wings. Wind in loose coils first the tinsel and then the hackle, and fasten both at the shoulder. Strip two wings from feathers that have been taken from the opposite sides of the bird, place them together, hold them firmly on the hook with the left forefinger and thumb, and fasten them securely; cut off the ends, insert a piece of herl, wind it over the head and tie it down. Lay the end of the silk back down the shank, and take three turns with the other part over silk, hook and gut; pass the gut end through the loop three times and draw the silk tight.

Two turns of silk should hold the different parts during the entire operation, and a couple of half hitches under the wings at the shoulders are sometimes used to fasten off, and the feathers should be mated to make neat wings; and if they are laid right side out they will close round the hook; if otherwise, they will stand out. Do not fail to varnish at the head with wood varnish, or some other kind that will dry rapidly. The hackle may be introduced at the shoulder. When herl or floss is used for the body, it is wound on separately from the tying silk, which is sometimes passed in open coils afterward. A second hackle of a different color, or a feather wound like a hackle, may be introduced after the first, or after the wings and before the head is finished, and is called the legs. The wings must be tied above the dubbing on the bare hook, or they will be liable to turn, especially where floss silk is used on the body. The following is a list of Canadian salmon flies:

No. 1, Louise.—An extremely beautiful fly, having wings composed of the golden pheasant's top-knot, breast feather and tail, with sprigs from the green parrot, blue macaw, and kingfisher; the body is fiery brown mohair, with gold twist; the head of orange mohair; the tail a single feather from the golden pheasant's top-knot; reddish brown hackle and jay legs.

No. 2, Edwin.—A much simpler fly, and often equally efficcaious among the fins, the wings being composed of the golden pheasant's tail feather, with a dash of yellow macaw; the body yellow mohair; ribs of black silk; head black mohair; tail, golden pheasant's top-knot; hackle yellow and scarlet silk tip.

No. 3, Forsyth.—Wings of the yellow macaw, with a slight dash of mallard wings at each side; yellow mohair body, with black ribs; head black; tail, golden pheasant's top-knot; hackle, yellow, with light blue silk tip.

No. 4, Stephens.—Wings of golden pheasant's breast feather, with slight mixture of mallard; body of reddish brick-colored silk, gold twist; head, black ostrich; tail, golden pheasant's top-knot; hackle, red, to match the body; tip blue silk.

No. 5, Ross.—Wings of mallard and peacock's herl; body, cinnamon-colored silk, gold twist; no head; tail, green parrot; red and black hackles and black tip.

No. 6, The Parson.—This is a beautiful and efficient fly; the wings are mixed, and very similar to those of No. 1, but have a slight mixture of wood duck in them; the body is of very dark claret silk, with gold twist; head, black ostrich; tail, golden pheasant's top-knot; hackle, dark claret; legs, blue, with a tip of yellow and gold.

No. 7, *Strachan.*—Mixed wings, chiefly of golden pheasant's tail; yellow macaw and jay's wings; body of crimson silk, with gold twist; head, black ostrich; tail golden pheasant; black hackle, with jay's wing legs; tip, yellow and gold.

No. 8, *Langevin.*—Wings, body, tail, hackle, legs, tip, all yellow, made of the dyed feathers of the white goose; the head of black ostrich, and the twist of black silk.

No. 9, *Whitcher.*—Mixed wings of mallard and shelldrake, or the tail of the golden pheasant may be used; head, black ostrich herl; black hackle and black mohair body, with a thin rib of silver; tip, yellow silk; and tail from the top-knot of the golden pheasant.

No. 10, *Grey Fly.*—Mixed wings, of mallard, turkey, golden pheasant's neck and top-knot, and sprigs of blue macaw; head of black ostrich herl; legs, carmine; grey hackle; body of a grey mohair, with silver ribs, and tip of silver and deep orange silk, tail, mixed gray mallard, and tail of the golden pheasant.

It will be observed that the foregoing are not imitations of any natural insects, but merely fanciful combinations of beautiful colors. The more harmonious the tints the finer the effect. Some of them are gaudy and for the rivers of New Brunswick I would add the following, requesting the reader to bear in mind that larger and more brilliant flies are permitted among the rougher waters and heavier fish of the Canadas.

No 11, *Nicholson.*—Wings, mallard with sprigs of blue macaw; body, blood-red mohair, head of black ostrich herl; hackles, one blood-red and one dark blue wound on together; gold ribs and tip, tail, mallard and golden pheasant neck. This is one of the best flies ever cast on the Miramichi and Nipisiquit, and is simple and inexpensive. It is often called "Blue and Brown."

No. 12, Chamberlain.—Turkey wing, the lighter and darker fibres mixed, or turkey and mallard; head, black ostrich herl; orange mohair, body and hackle; yellow legs; silver or gold ribs and tip, black silk twist; tail of golden pheasant top knot.

No. 13, Darling.—Wings of turkey, and golden pheasant neck feather and sprigs of blue macaw; head black ostrich; hackles black along the stem, but with reddish ends sometimes called "fiery brown;" tip orange silk; tail golden pheasant top knot; thin gold ribs and tag and black mohair body.

No. 14, Major.—Wings of mallard and turkey with sprigs of blue macaw; head claret herl; light red hackle, and orange legs; body deep purple mohair; tip blue silk; tail, golden pheasant neck feathers, ribs and tag gold tinsel.

No. 15, Captain.—Wings of turkey and golden pheasant, tail and neck feathers and sprigs of blue macaw; head, claret herl; red hackle; body, claret mohair; tip, orange silk; silver tag, gold ribs and tail of golden pheasant top knot.

No. 16, Ceriboo.—Wings of turkey and mallard with sprigs of macaw, and a few fibres from the golden pheasant's neck, head of black ostrich herl; claret legs; grey hackle, body of green cariboo hair or mohair, lower part of tip golden yellow silk, and upper part black silk; tail, golden pheasant top-knot, and gold tag. This fly, with various modifications, is extensively used by the resident fishermen of Frederickton.

No. 17, Emmet.—No head; wings of black and golden pheasant neck feather with sprigs of macaw; body, black mohair; black hackle; gold tip and twist; a turn of black herl taken just above the tail, which is golden pheasant crest.

No. 18, *Lillie*—Wings and tail dark grey turkey; body, mohair of the same dull color; yellow silk tip; red hackle and no head.

We have given more particular directions about salmon than trout flies because the comparative number is smaller, and it is more difficult for one of our people to ascertain correctly what flies he will need in Canada and the British Provinces, and if he makes a mistake he cannot easily correct it and may be put to considerable inconvenience by finding himself in the heart of the wilderness by the side of a salmon river and with a book full of unsuitable flies. The above are all, and we might say, more than all that will be needed on any river on the Atlantic coast of America, and they will answer as well on the Pacific coast rivers as any flies yet discovered.

There is one fact to be borne in mind in reference to all flies, either for trout or salmon, and that is, that fish get accustomed to any kind of artificial lure, which must be changed from time to time. One fly, no matter how good, will lose its attraction. Many anglers have from a season's good luck concluded that they have at last discovered the fly of flies until the failures of next year convinced them that their favorite was no better than its fellows. Anything odd, out of the way or unusual will receive more or less attention, especially from salmon, when every ordinary fly has been tried in vain. We have made a new fly, and with the most startling colors we had at hand, every day for weeks in midsummer when salmon fishing in clear low water in pools that had been well whipped for a couple of months, and on such occasions were sure to raise several fish with every new fly, that lost its virtues, however, before the day was out.

A simple arrangement for quickly changing the color of a fly, especially with trout flies, which have not such brilliantly colored wings as salmon flies, is to carry in the fly book cards with various colored silks wound upon them. There will be no difficulty in having as many as thirty varieties of shade because only a little is needed of each and they may be placed side by side so that any hue may be selected at once. It is a good plan to open the first trout taken and find out from the contents of his stomach the precise fly on which he is feeding. Then if the angler is without that kind he can make a tolerable substitute by winding the proper shade of silk over the body of any fly that he has, selecting suitable size and wings as far as he can. It is the color of the body that mainly distinguishes trout flies and the wings are of less importance, being in nature little more than a dusky membrane.

REELS.—There is probably no better reel than the ordinary click reel. It should have the handle set in the plate and not on an arm around which the line will be forever catching. For salmon fishing of course, the reel must be larger and stronger than for trout. The advantage about the ordinary brass reel is, that it will not break if it falls even on rocks, a misfortune that is peculiarily liable to happen in salmon fishing, in which the fish have often to be followed along a dangerous and difficult shore. It may get bent, but it can still be used. The objections to it are, that it keeps the line shut in between two plates, so that it will not dry readily and may rot, and that it does not take in the line rapidly. An open reel with a large barrel, and made of gutta percha has come into vogue lately. It will wind in the line far more quickly than the ordinary click reel, and when wound in, leaves it in such a position that it will dry, but if this reel strikes any hard substance heavily, it will fly to pieces, being as brittle as an ordinary gutta percha comb, and it does not yield the line nicely to the hand when the angler is lengthening his casts, the line binding on the narrow slit through which it runs. This reel may be made with a click or a friction screw, and should be sold very cheaply. We have used it for years in trout fishing, and cannot say that we give the old brass click reel any preference over it, and it certainly enables us to command the line more quickly when we have hooked a fish. We have not, however, as yet, slammed it against a rock, an experience that is reserved for the first time we lose our footing on the slimy, treacherous bottom of the trout brook we may be wading.

CASTING THE FLY.—We can think of no way of giving oral or written instruction in fly fishing. The purpose is to get the line out straight, clear and lightly as far as possible, and skill in doing so is only to be acquired with practice. Something can be learned by watching a better angler than yourself standing and casting by your side. The motion is a peculiar one, and the best advice we can give the reader about it is, to tell him to send his line out with a jerk. This is contrary to every opinion and direction contained in the books, and will at first, lead to the snapping off of many a fly, but it is the only way of casting the line as it should be cast. Every other plan will work after a fashion if there is a breeze to favor and help, but on calm water and with no wind, it is only the man that can twitch out his line that can get it out at all. We should say lift it with a jerk, swing it to the full length behind you; upon doing this thoroughly, depends the question whether your fly will stay on the line or not, and then send it forward with a quick motion that winds up with a jerk of the wrist. This jerk communicates itsself to the tip, and gives that peculiar springy motion that will be noticed with all first-class fly fishermen. Never try to help your rod by a long, slow awkward sweep of the arm. It won't answer—the wrist must do the work. Do not let your rod go too far back, it should never reach more than an angle of forty-five degrees. And now, reader, if these directions don't suit you, you need not follow them, they are poor enough at best, and you may work out your own fishing salvation in your own way. If they do, and you will courageously snap off about fifty flies, we think at the end of that time you can probably cast a line fifty feet long, and drop your tail fly in a lily pad three times in five casts, in which case you can begin to take trout.

Fish have sharp eyes, and in trying to allure them to their death we must do our best to keep out of their sight. They know a man as their natural enemy by instinct. In approaching a stream, get behind a bush, or stump, or rock. We have before now crawled on our knees within reach of a hole in which we knew that a peculiarly large and desirable trout had taken up his abode. In fishing from a boat, always sit down and have the seats arranged to face towards the stern. Omit no precautions that will tend to lull the suspicions of the trout, which years of persecution have rendered most acute. Never pound on the bottom of the boat, or jar the bank of the creek. Talking will do no harm, but rattling oars or jumping from one log to another, or splashing in the water, or even treading heavily on the ground will alarm the fish and often make them dart about in terror. When once alarmed, trout will never bite. It is worse than useless to show them bait or fly, and only teaches them to connect in their minds the noise and the fishing.

OTHER METHODS OF FISHING.—As salmon and trout are only taken for sport, they should never be caught with anything but the fly, which is the highest development of sport in fishing. Salmon are never fished for in any other way, but it will occasionally happen that a trout stream is so overgrown with trees and bushes, that the use of the fly is an impossibility. In such cases a person is perfectly justified in having resort to a worm. For this kind of work, especially in the small brooks which are so common in our country, and which flow down some mountain side through dense and unbroken woods, the best rod is a pole cut from the forest, as it can be taken by the smaller end and dragged along, when more delicate tackle would give trouble. The best line is a gut leader, which is tied to the end of the pole, and may be shortened by turning the latter in the hands and winding it up. For larger streams, where a reel can be used, a short rod with a small float are the proper implements. Pay out as much line, and keep the float as far ahead as possible; have a leader of two or three feet in length, and no sinker. In streams connected with salt water and in ponds, minnows are better bait than worms. Minnows and worms can both be cast and played somewhat like the fly, and often with deadly effect.

Trolling spoons are fatal with the larger sea trout of Canada, and may either be drawn along after the boat while it is being rowed, or if small enough, they may be cast like the fly. It is rather a coarse method of fishing, and if a fish is once hooked he can never escape, except by breaking the line, as the hooks of the spoon will be imbedded in his jaws so that they are difficult of extraction after he is landed. Such devices are more appropriate to fishing for pickerel or mascallonge, than for so delicate and beautiful a fish as the trout. Artificial minnows, artificial grasshoppers, and the like, are not successful enough to justify their use.

SALMON-TROUT.—As the fishing for salmon-trout is altogether different from that for salmon or trout, we will give separate directions in reference to it. These fish are known under several names, both scientific and popular; but it is questionable whether there are more than two species. In different waters they have a distinct appearance and differ greatly in size, but it is doubtful whether the changes are more than the mere effect of local causes. They are fond of large sheets of water, the smallest of which, and where they attain the least growth, deserving the name of lakes. In such inland seas as Lake Superior, they will occasionally reach a weight of one hundred pounds, while in other places they will not average over two or three. They are common in most of the northern and north-western ponds and lakes, and are a favorite food fish with many. They are taken with silver and brass spoon hooks, by loading the line so that the spoon runs near the bottom. But they are taken sometimes at the top of the water, and sometimes half-way down, and at the bottom, by trolling with three lines at one time —one at the surface, one half-way down, and one near the bottom. Another way is to anchor a buoy out in deep water and cut fish in pieces, varying in size from a hickorynut to a butternut, and scatter the pieces around the buoy for some days; then anchor your boat to the buoy, using a piece of the same kind of bait on your hook that you had been in the habit of scattering around your buoy; fish near the bottom, and give it a little motion by giving your line short jerks. The buoy should not be baited the day you go fishing.

Another way is to have a rod and reel and four or five hundred feet of fine, strong line, and if the water is deep put a lead sinker weighing three quarters of a pound on the end of your line, and tie a single gut leader twelve feet long, on the main line twelve feet above your sinker. For hooks, you should use nine number six Limerick hooks, tied three together, back to back, so that they look like a three-pronged grappel. Tie them on a single gut leader about two and one-half inches apart, and you have a gang of hooks five inches long. Put two very small brass swivels on your leader. Use the kind of small fish for bait that the trout are used to eating in your lake. Hook one of the upper hooks through the under and upper jaw so that his mouth will be closed; then hook one of the lower hooks through the back near the tail, in such a manner that it will give the fish a curve and will turn around like a trolling-spoon when it is drawn through the water. The most successful fishermen use three of these kind of rigs in one boat; they fish one rig near the top with a light sinker, say four ounces, and one about half-way down with an eight ounce sinker, and the twelve ounce sinker near the bottom. The boat should be rowed very slowly, so that you can feel the bottom with the heavy sinker nearly every time you raise it up and let it down. The bait should be raised up and down by a gentle motion; set the other two lines, one on each side of the boat, and they will take care of themselves. Live fish should be used for bait. Some do not use but eight hooks, one hook for the upper to hook in the minnow's mouth, and one to hook in the back near the tail, and two sets of three each between the two single hooks tied about one and-a-half inches apart. Be careful and keep your minnow looking as natural as possible. Do not rub any more scales off than you can help. When you let your line out your boat should be in motion to keep your bait from twisting around the main line.

There is opportunity for fine fishing in Lake Huron, which will be utilized one of these days when yachting shall have been developed in our grand inland lakes, as it will be in time. Trolling for salmon-trout can be done very successfully with sailing craft, all the way from Saginaw Bay to Mackinaw, and about five or ten miles from shore. The ordinary trolling tackle is to be used, much in the same way that it is used on the sea coast for blue fish, but the fish taken will occasionally exceed twenty pounds in weight, and will test the angler's tackle and muscles.

CHAPTER XVI.

FISHING FOR BASS AND OTHER FISH.

BLACK BASS.—These fish are taken with the fly either cast as in trout fishing or trolled behind a boat and with spinning tackle. They are also caught with bait and show a preference for fresh water helgramite and crawfish and, for small living roach, dace and yellow perch. They are a voracious and predacious fish and will destroy any other kind that occupies any small waters with them, even the pickerel standing no chance against them. They are courageous as well, and never give up their lives till after they have made a good fight. As soon as they are hooked they throw themselves out of the water with a rush and endeavor to smash the line, and shake their heads fiercely in their attempts to dislodge the hook. When they jump out of the water it is well to drop the tip, as, if they succeed in flinging their broad sides on the line, they are apt either to snap it or tear out the hook. They must be handled carefully and cannot be landed immediately, and if they are of any considerable size will demand skillful play. They attain a weight of six to eight pounds, but the average is far less, hardly exceeding two. They are thoroughly a game fish and should be introduced into all waters adapted for them which are occupied by inferior fish.

There is scarcely any prettier sport than taking black bass by casting the fly. Trolling is far inferior in the enjoyment it gives the true angler, being a coarser and less artistic style of fishing. For very large fish the leader may be of salmon gut, but for ordinary fish, trout tackle will do. In trolling a number of flies of light colors, especially scarlet and white, are tied on the leader at short intervals with often a small trolling spoon for a stretcher. It should have a swivel at the top and a couple of shot lower down. This is trailed behind at some distance from the boat which is rowed rather slowly over the reefs and other places where the bass congregate. In the St Lawrence river among the Thousand Isles where a school of these fish is struck every fly will hook a fish and the fortunate spot may be crossed again and again with the same result. This is a good deal like pot fishing however, and the landing of so many fish at one time is annoying rather than pleasurable. As they fight against one another, success in getting them into the net is a question rather of strength of tackle than of skill in the fisherman.

In casting this is wholly different and everything depends on ability to use the rod and to manage the game. The flies are larger ordinarily than those for trout being about the size of such as are used in Maine or on Lake Superior, and are gaudy although on light days sombre colors are often the most successful. Otherwise there is no essential difference between fly fishing for black bass and for trout, except that it is well to fish a little more slowly. The rod is the same, the line the same, and there is the same necessity for dexterity in controlling the fly and the line. Black bass are not so beautiful nor delicate a fish, but they are more fierce and fully as courageous. They are rarely brought to the net till after they have leaped a half dozen times from the water, sometimes as high as three feet from its surface. The thrill of dread which this manœuvre on their part arouses in the mind of the fisherman is never staled by repetition and there is no assurance of safety till the bass is fairly landed.

Oswego Bass.—These fish resemble the black bass so closely that they are often confounded with them, but they are quite inferior. They inhabit a lower class of waters, prefering ponds and streams with sluggish currents and muddy bottoms. They rarely rise to the fly but will take the trolling spoon voraciously. When hooked, however, they make no play but after one or two feeble rushes come in like a "wet rag." Neither are they so good a table fish as the black bass. They inhabit most of the southern waters of our country being found in vast numbers in the coast lagoons of the southern states, in water that is often quite blackish from the inroads of the sea during high tides. They grow to weigh fifteen pounds quite frequently and sometimes are said to exceed that by as much as five more. In the northern states they rarely exceed five or six pounds.

Mascallonge.—This fish, which is the king of the pickerel tribe, grows to a great size and gives good sport. He is strong and willful, and is much better on the table than his smaller kinsmen. He is taken by trolling with a row-boat and what is known as the trolling spoon,—a piece of tin wheeling around a pair of hooks. Sometimes feathers are tied around the shank of the hooks, and while the outside or face of the tin has its natural shining color, the back is sometimes made red, sometimes black or copper colored, and so forth. We prefer the trolling spoon without feathers for mascallonge, but we often use a double gang of hooks and put a piece of the throat of the fish on the lower pair. Then if the fish strikes and does not hook himself, he gets a taste of food and will often come again. In case minnow is used either for mascallonge or pickerel, it is fastened on a gang of small hooks that are thrust into its back and sides so as to bend it in order that it may turn round and round in the water,—" spin well" as it is technically termed.

PICKEREL AND YELLOW PERCH.—The most artistic way of taking pickerel in summer is with the spear, but they are generally taken with a spoon and line bait. They furnish poor food and worse sport, as a general thing, and are not entitled to any law. They are better to use as food for black bass than for man. During winter they and perch are caught through the ice in a way to furnish a good deal of amusement. A number of holes are cut through the ice some distance apart, and two sticks tacked together in the shape of a cross are laid across each hole. The longest part of the cross reaches over to the ice on both sides, but the other piece is too short to strike the edges. To one end of the latter the line is made fast, and as soon as a fish bites his jerk raises the other end, which can be seen at some distance, and may be decorated with a tiny flag. The fisherman is kept running from one to another, and as he has from twenty-five to fifty lines fishing all the while, he is busy if fish are at all plentiful. A similar method of fishing may be followed in summer by having a flat float of a piece of ordinary board with a stick run up and down through the center and weighted at the bottom. The line is fastened to the upper end, that half being painted white, and a bite reverses the position and shows the lower half, which is painted red. As pickerel do not always pouch the bait when they first strike it, the line may be coiled on the float and slightly hitched in a notch so that it will run off at first and give the pickerel a chance to move to a quiet spot for his deliberate meal. For this fishing, live bait is needed, minnows being the best, and should be fastened by running the hook just under the skin near the back fin, so as not to injure them. If the line is tied to the leg of a tame goose, there will be seen considerable excitement when this new sort of angler strikes a large fish. Pickerel are also taken in small ponds, where they love to lie around the water lilies and long grass, by fishing for them with a long rod and small fish. The bait is tossed here and there into the openings among the weeds, is twitched up and down in a way to somewhat simulate the action of a living fish. When a fish bites he is unceremoniously hauled out.

SHAD FLY-FISHING.—Shad can be taken with the fly, but only where they are collected together in considerable quantities, or over a reef, or where they are obstructed by a dam or falls. The same rule obtains with salmon, which never rise to the fly in smooth, still water, and are caught most freely where the fresh stream falls directly by rapids or cataract into the brackish or salt tideway. If the lower part of the river is unbroken, the salmon run directly up and are never taken by fly-fishing, and if they have to ascend a long distance to the first rough water, they do not rise so well. It is possible that the failure of salmon to take the fly in the Columbia and other streams of Oregon and California, is due to the fact that the falls are so far from the ocean, and they might possibly be made to rise by an artificial obstruction.

The ordinary fly used in fishing for shad is one that is a dull yellow throughout, the color of the sandhoppers that are found on the sandy shores of salt water. It is trolled more generally than cast, and has been used successfully in the Connecticut and Hudson rivers. The sport, however, is not such as to attract the thorough fisherman, and has been pursued rather from curiosity than for amusement. Shad have been taken in fresh water with the minnow.

STRIPED BASS.—The fishing for striped bass is altogether different from anything that has heretofore been described. It requires a different rod, reel, line and bait. It is true that at certain places bass may be taken with a large coarse fly either cast or used in trolling, but these spots are so rare that but few anglers have ever enjoyed the sport of fly fishing for striped bass. The best place for this is at the Little Falls of the Potomac, and the sportsmen of Washington are favored in having the privilege. But in general the fishing for striped bass is done with bait and a rod that is short, strong but springy, not over nine feet in length but very stiff by comparison with anything used for salmon or trout. The finest rods are made with the second joint and tip—there are only three joints—of bamboo, and the butt of some heavier wood. A single piece of Japanese bamboo makes an excellent rod and may be had at a cheap price but it is awkward to carry. The guides which are used in place of rings, and tip point or "funnel top," should be lined with agate in order that the line may run through them with the utmost freedom, this being the great desideratum in the more difficult kinds of bass fishing.

More important even than the rod is the reel. This must be made with the delicacy of the finest clock work. It is a multiplier and should either run on agates or steel pins, the latter is not so easily broken as the former and renders as well if it is kept well oiled. The cog wheels must be as perfect as they can be and run with absolute accuracy and noiselessness. The least jar or chatter renders the whole thing utterly useless. The handle is balanced and the main barrel is large and able to hold three hundred yards of line. When a good reel has once been selected it needs and deserves the best of care; it should be kept in a leather case, and if it is unused for some time should be oiled occasionally. Before it is used and when it is about being put away it should be taken apart, wiped dry and oiled, and all rust must be thoroughly removed.

LINES AND LEADERS.—The best lines are of grass or raw silk, but they are expensive, rot easily, require the utmost care, and will whip out against the bars of the reel. Silk lines are apt to stick and will not deliver rapidly, and custom has fallen upon those of flax. These are poor affairs at best; they swell when wet and rot unless they are dried after every wetting, but they are the most practical taken all in all, that the tackle makers have yet given us. From twelve to fifteen threads are the sizes generally used, although some persons prefer those of eighteen. Of course the finer the line the sooner it looses its strength, and deteriorates under exposure. No bass fisherman can do himself justice with any line but one of raw silk, and the question only is whether he can afford—taking into consideration his purse and the amount of fishing he may do—to buy the best or whether he must content himself with inferior tackle at a moderate price. Even a poor fisherman can make a fair show with a grass line, while a good one will often have his patience tried with a line of flax.

These costly and delicate implements are only needed for the higher kinds of bass fishing and for the largest sized fish. For smaller fish and smaller sport, lighter tackle will answer, but when the fish has the entire Atlantic ocean to escape into, and the angler expects, prays and hopes for a victim to his skill of fifty pounds weight it is unwise to use any but the best and strongest tackle. In the innumerable salt water creeks, coves and bays where fish of from three to five pounds are taken, a plain rod with a float and sinker and double snell of hooks on gut leaders is all that is necessary. More will be said on this subject hereafter.

The grandest and most skilful method of taking the striped beauties of the northern coasts, is with the menhaden bait, cast into the boiling surf of the ocean, or the larger bays, and this sport is universally enjoyed along the rock bound coast of New England, from New London to Eastport. This entire beach is one mass of rock indented by innumerable bays or severed by inlets into barren islands, where the tide rushes and the surf beats, and in every favorable locality are the bass taken with a stout rod, a long line and menhaden bait. From almost every bold rock, or prominent island can the angler cast into the vexed water of some current made by the waves rushing over the uneven bottom, and allure thence the bass, who has been attracted from the ocean depths to feed on the small fry that hide in the clefts and crevices, and waiting with fins often visible above the tide to pounce upon his prey, mistakes for it the angler's bait, and after a brave struggle surrenders to human ingenuity.

Fishermen of long practice and great skill claim that they can cast the ordinary menhaden bait one hundred and twenty yards. Although from a high stand with the aid of a strong wind this is possible, the ordinary cast is not over half that distance, and to exceed one hundred when standing on a level with the water is rare. Seventy five yards is a good cast, and no man need be ashamed who can put out his line fair and true that distance. The length of cast is in a measure controlled by the direction and violence of the wind and the elevation of the stand above the water. In a contrary wind the best angler will find it difficult to reach seventy-five yards, while from a high rock with a favorable wind he will cover that distance with ease.

Casting the menhaden bait is similar to casting the float and sinker, only the power applied is enormously increased, and difficulties are proportionally magnified. The line is wound up till the bait, if a single one, is almost two feet from the tip, the rod is extended behind the fisherman, who turns his body for the purpose, and then brought forward with a steady but vigorous swing that discharges it without a jerk, like an apple thrown from a stick. The reel is so far restrained by pressure of the thumb, that it revolves no faster than the bait travels, but does not detain it, and upon the accuracy of this manipulation mainly depends the result. If too much pressure is used, the line cannot escape rapidly enough and falls short; if too little, the reel overruns and entangles the line, stopping the cast ere half delivered with a jerk that threatens its destruction. The fisherman must be able to use either hand on the reel to rest his arms and to take advantage of the wind.

Neither shrimp nor soft crabs are used in this style of fishing, and the eel skin which is used earlier in the season, is prepared by stripping the skin off the tail of an eel from the vent aft for about a foot, turn it inside out, and drawing it over a couple of hooks so placed on the line that one shall project, near the upper and the other near the tail end. A sinker of the size of one's little finger is inserted at the head, and this bait is cast by hand, as it has to be drawn rapidly. The rod is not often used in this style of fishing, as the heavy bait is apt to sink ere it can be reeled in. The skin is frequently salted to increase its firmness, and when used, must be kept in continual motion.

The menhaden bait is prepared by scaling it and then cutting a slice on one side from near the head to the base of the tail, passing the hook through from the scaly side, and back through both edges, so that the shank is enveloped and the flesh is outwards, and then tying the bait firmly with a small piece of twine that is attached to the hook for that purpose. A menhaden or bony fish furnishes two baits and the residue, except the back bone, tail, and head, is cut up fine, called chum, and thrown into the water to make a slick. A slick is the oil of the menhaden floating over the waves, and being carried by the tide or current a long distance, attracts the bass.

Where the water is clear, it is customary in rod-fishing, to use two hooks; the smaller some two feet below the other is attached to a fine line or gut leader, which latter we decidedly recommend, and denominated without any apparent reason the "fly hook." Many of the best fishermen never use more than one bait, and when the fish are large and plenty, one is sufficient. The fly bait is not generally tied on, but twisted round the hook in a manner difficult to describe.

Lobster which is also used as a bait in this style of fishing is deficient in tenacity, and has to be tied on like menhaden, and probably the natural squid would be an effective and manageable bait, could it be provided in sufficient quanities. Hooks are manufactured expressly for this fishing with a round head, they are fastened to the line with two half hitches, the end again hitched above so as to take the friction; and as they are carried off by the first big blue fish or in the Yankee vernacular horse-mackerel, that takes a fancy to the bait the angler must be well supplied.

The friction is so great in casting, that the thumb must be protected by a thumb stall or " cot," as fishermen call it, or better yet, one for each thumb, so that you can cast from either side, and snub the fish with either hand. They are made of chamois, leather, india rubber, or some equivalent material, and in casting by hand, a similar protection is required for the forefinger. A shoemaker's knife is admirably adapted to cutting bait, and the best tool is desirable, as cutting up monhaden bait is about as dirty, disagreeable and tedious an operation as can be imagined. The angler should always have an assistant for the purpose, or he will get his hands, his rod, and his clothes in a condition of oil, blood and fish scales, that no cleaning will wholly remove, and his person will smell "ancient and fish-like" for weeks.

Bass fishermen will boast that they never allow their lines to over run, but listeners should make allowances for sportsmen's stories. We all like to believe that we can shoot and fish as well as the best or a little better, and ambition to excel is laudable. The truth is, there never was a fisherman yet whose line did not sometimes over-run and foul. This occurrence is the drawback to the sport, and there seems to be no way of preventing it. The pressure to be applied to the reel depends upon so many considerations, the force and direction of the wind, the power applied to the cast, the speed of the bait which diminishes as it progresses, and the quality of the line and perfect working of the reel, whereby the restraining tension is so difficult to apply perfectly, so hard to regulate exactly to the occasion—that no angler, however skillful or experienced can always be sure that his line will go out clean and clear, without bagging or catching, while at the same time his bait reaches the utmost limit of distance to which he can drive it.

So much for bass fishing in the surf, a sport that compares favorably with and is only surpassed by salmon fishing; but we must not neglect the smaller run of these fish which are taken by rod and reel, from the weight of eight ounces to that of sixty pounds. The large fish are diminishing at so rapid a rate that there is danger that before many years have passed surf fishing will have ceased to be practiced, and Cuttyhunk, Pasque and West Island will be deserted, as Point Judith is already. Far more persons are interested in the milder sport, and there is hope that it will last until the time comes when bass will be bred artificially as trout and salmon now are, and when a stop shall be put to the decrease of these fish.

The prettiest mode of taking striped bass must be admitted to be with the fly, which, unfortunately can only be done in the brackish or fresh water. Like salmon, they will not take the fly generally in the salt creeks and bays, and then only when it is trolled. Thus though the sport of fly fishing for striped bass is excellent, it is confined to few localities, and those often difficult of access. Fly fishing may be done either with the ordinary salmon rod, or in a strong current with a common bass rod, by working your fly on the top of the water and giving a considerable length of line. The best fly is that with the scarlet ibis and white feathers mixed, the same as used for black bass; but bass may be taken with any large fly, especially those of the Blue Jay color. Excellent sport is occasionally had in this way from off some open bridge, where the falling tide mixed with the fresh water rushes furiously between the piers. In other streams striped bass are taken early in the season with shrimp threaded on the hook, by passing the point under the back plates; as the season advances and crabs shed their coats, with the shedder crabs, and in the fall with shrimp, the barred killey and the spearing.

In fishing with shrimp—and it is a good bait all the season through and must be tried when others fail—use a float fastened about three feet above a swivel sinker, to the lower swivel of which are to be attached two distinct gut leaders, one of three feet, the other of two. Single gut, if large, round and true, is decidedly preferable, and the hook should have a broad, round bend. If very large fish are expected—and they rarely are—use No. 0, but generally No, 3 is large enough. With crab the hook must be larger. We prefer always to have the point of the hook covered, and recommend that the shrimp should be bunched on till they hide the hook entirely, and form a round, attractive bait. In June, and throughout the summer the crab is a better bait ordinarily than the shrimp.

There is no unbending rule for fishing; the only way is to try all plans, and if the fish will not notice your crab suspended in mid-water, take off your float and swivel sinker, put on a running sinker, as it is called, made like a piece of lead pipe, with a small hole in the center, tie a knot in the line to prevent its going down on the hooks; use a single bait of a good sized piece of crab, and cast well out from you, and let the bait lie still till you feel a bite. The line being free, though the lead lies on the bottom, you can feel the first touch of a fish and can strike at once, whereas if the sinker were the old-fashioned deep sea lead, he would have to drag its weight some distance before you were aware of his proceedings. The angler, by fishing on the bottom, although justified by a philosophy which establishes the fact that bass ought to look for crabs there, and not dangling about in mid-water, will surely catch three eels to one bass. The bait except when on the bottom, should be kept in continual motion; this is the first law of all bait fishing. It is done by twitching the rod, and induces the fish to seize the prey, which they imagine is about to escape. Every angler has seen the fish time and again dart at a bait when in motion, that they smelt round contemptuously when still. Crab is generally regarded as the pre-eminent bass bait in summer, although some anglers prefer that wonderful product of the sea, the squid.

As the days grow colder, and the crab re-assumes his impenetrable coat and dangerous pincers, shrimp again come into play, and on many occasions the belly of the white soft clam will attract the bass even earlier in the season. But in August excellent sport is had casting, if we may use the word, for him with the spearing. Early in the summer, a delicate little fish, an inch or two long, pearly white and semi-transparent, with a black eye and a white band along the lateral line, makes its appearance on the shores of Long Island and elsewhere, and has come to be called the spearing. It is a beautiful fish, and properly dressed might rival in delicacy the English white-bait, but it is never brought to market till later in the season, when it has grown several inches long and is comparatively tasteless. Being too small in the early summer to take a hook, they are difficult to catch; but a good working net, both for these and killey-fish, can be made of mosquito netting stretched double between two hoop poles, with a stout cord run along the top and bottom to receive the leads and floats respectively. The netting being wide can be doubled together with the lead line laid in the bag, or, as sailors would say of a rope, in the "bight"; and the leads being small bits of pipe, fastened at short intervals, will keep the net close to the bottom —an important particular. It should be five to six yards long, and two men taking each a handle, can sweep a considerable part of the shore, and often fill a pail with minnows or spearing at one haul. The killey-fish, so called by our ancestors from being caught in the "kills" or creeks, and of which there are at least three common kinds, will rush about and try to creep under the net, but spearing go in shoals, and when once in the net do not seem to be able to escape, but will stay there as long as it is kept in motion. If spearing cannot be had, though that is rare, the barred killey, vulgarly called the bass killey, is the next in beauty and attractiveness, and if it cannot be had the ugly green killey-fish may be used, or the shrimp itself.

To cast with spearing in the manner here suggested, successfully, a stout, long salmon rod will be requisite. A small hook is run through the spearing's mouth, and out at his side, for he dies quickly and cannot be used alive, and a cast is made into the foaming torrent of a mill-tail or rushing tide. The bait is drawn irregularly over the surface of the water, and again cast and played like the fly. The bass strike it as trout or salmon take the latter, and there is much the same skill and uncertainty in the pursuit. In fishing with the killey, it is usual to keep him alive by merely running the hook under his skin alongside of the back fin. He will live for hours under such treatment.

BLUE FISH.—These fish furnish one of the most remarkable instances of the appearance and disappearance of species on our coast. As in our day with the Spanish mackerel, that favorite of the gourmand, so in former times the blue fish appeared suddenly. He was first seen on the coast of Massachusetts in 1764, and then not again till 1792, and it is only since the year 1830 that he has been abundant. He seems to have superseded another and larger fish of the same name, and as his numbers augment, those of the weak fish diminish. The blue fish has singular vagaries, sometimes crowding every inlet in swarms, and then deserting us altogether, visiting in one season one locality, and in the next another, but ordinarily frequenting our entire coast north to Massachusetts. They afford excellent sport on a rod and line, being among the strongest and boldest of their kind, taking the fly readily under certain circumstances, and they fight well when hooked, but from the character of the localities they usually frequent, they are mostly taken with a hand line from a sail boat. An artificial squid of bone ivory or lead is trailed along at the end of forty yards of stout line from a boat dancing merrily over the waves under the influences of a moderate breeze. The boatman's business is to watch for a shoal which can be seen by their breaking in their pursuit of the mossbunkers or by the action of the gulls, and when he has found it, by repeated tacks to keep the boat in or near it, the fisherman's duty is to haul in steadily and regularly immediately on feeling a bite, and to get out his line again as soon as possible. The fish dart forward when hooked and throwing themseves out of water turn almost a complete somersault, when, if the line is not taut, they will throw the hook out of their mouths. The dashing of the waves and flying of the spray, the rapid exhilarating motion of the vessel, the fresh sea breeze, the rapid biting, and fine play of the fish make a day pass pleasantly in trolling for blue fish.

A variety of squids is desirable, for dark days the bright one are preferable and for bright days the contrary, but for general use the leaden or pewter squid is the best. The size must be adapted to that of the fish. After a run of good fish in the latter part of May none appear in our bays until about July first when the small ones arrive. For these small squids are desirable, but as the season advances and they grow larger the bait also must be larger. Their teeth are sharp and will cut through the line if they reach above the hook, and it is said, will take off the fisherman's finger if he puts it in their mouths. It is necessary to have a stout line, and it is well also to wear gloves to prevent cutting the hands, the shearing about of the fish together with the motion of the boat causing sharp jerks and a heavy strain, and when the water is clear and the fish shy it will be found profitable to use a twisted or double gut leader for a short distance above the squid. This will stand a good pull and will lift an ordinary fish out of water, and if one is occasionally carried off will more than pay for itself by the extra number of bites that it will obtain. There are no shyer fish than blue fish, fierce and ravenous as they are. It they encounter the wing of a pound net on entering a harbor they will not attempt to pass around it like bass and weak fish and even Spanish mackerel but they will turn back immediately and go out to sea again. The finer the tackle that can be used with them the more successful the fisherman will be, and throughout the entire summer months no blue fish will be encountered that cannot be hauled into a boat on a good line of double salmon gut. Beyond this there is not much science in trolling for blue fish, although there is some practice necessary in keeping one's feet on the deck of the yacht, if a yacht is used, while it is dashing over the waves of the ocean and the fisherman's attention is absorbed in hauling in his line more rapidly than the fastest of fish can swim forward on it.

Still fishing for blue fish has become quite a favorite sport lately in localities where formerly nothing but trolling was ever thought of. There is an excitement in dancing over the restless ocean in the diminutive sail boat; there is more or less of danger upon the "mighty deep" and passing in and out of the angry, sullen, threatening inlet, with its rows upon rows of crested breakers, its uncertain and changing shoals and its rapid currents, and there is always the possibility of being caught out all night by the turning of the tide or the falling of the wind. So that although the mere striking and hauling in the fish on a stout line and with a big hook would otherwise be dull sport, the accompaniments make trolling more exhilarating than bait fishing from an anchored vessel. The sport has, however, so greatly deteriorated of late the fish have become so scarce, being caught by pound nets placed across their favorite inlets or by fishing with fly nets at night on their feeding grounds inside the lagoons along the coast, that trolling with a sail boat, at least near New York has almost ceased to furnish remuneration either in the way of sport or profit, and anglers have been driven to other methods. One of the best of these is still fishing with rod and reel.

The same tackle is used as in bass fishing in the surf, except that the hook had better be fastened to the line with a length of fine brass wire to prevent the saw shaped teeth of the blue fish cutting it off. The boat is anchored generally in the channel, inside of the inlet where there is a strong current, but often out in the ocean itself. Menhaden, otherwise called mossbunkers or bony-fish are used for bait. A number of these fish are cut in pieces and cast into the water to make what is called a "slick"—the oil from them floating on the surface. This is continued until the blue fish are attracted and are tolled in to take the food. The angler then baiting his hook with mossbunker commences his work. Casting into the strong current his bait is carried off as far as he cares to let it go, and amid the "chum" as the chopped fish is called. As it offers a more attractive morsel than the smaller pieces around it, a blue fish is sure to give it the preference, and

> Darting upon it with hungry maw,
> He sinks the hook in his upper jaw.

Then comes " a terrible rush of fear and dread with a force by rage made double," and away goes the fish and out runs the line till the reel sings " sweetest music to attendant ears," and the fisherman has all he can do to control and conquer his powerful prey. Blue fish are game from the tips of their noses to the ends of their caudal fins, and have back bone for anything. They are worthy relatives of the dolphin, of antique and lyric fame. They fight to the last, and in their dying gasps do not disdain to bite off the finger or thumb of their victor if he comes "fooling around" their jaws too heedlessly. Such sport as this is not to be despised, and compares fairly with that had with a "wet sheet and a flowing sea." It is followed at Fire Island inlet on Long Island and elsewhere, and will be successful in any water inhabited by blue fish, where there is a current and where bait can be obtained. Formerly a weak imitation of it was indulged in by Miss Nancy fishermen who regarded trolling with a hand line as coarse work, and who had themselves towed in a row boat behind a sail boat while they fished with rod and reel. As soon as they struck a fish it was the duty of one of the hands on the sail boat to cast them loose and let them kill it at their leisure. They could not fish from the sail boat because its speed added to that of the fish was more than their tackle would stand. Such make-believe sport however never had many followers, and still fishing, such as we have described has wholly supplanted it and is in every way to be preferred.

The sport "outside" is better than that inside the inlet, as the fish are larger and there is something glorious in fishing in the clear depths and on the limitless surface of the mighty ocean, but we warn all who have the least tendency to sea sickness to avoid it. When anchored "amid the breakers," the boat, whether large or small, rolls, pitches, twists, turns, wobbles and dances in a way that is wholly unexpected even by those who have had experience on the unstable element, and good sailors have become so sick in a short time that they have scarcely been able to get up their anchors, make sail and work back again into smooth water. In all chumming there are but two secrets; cut the chum fine, and use enough of it. Although we have spoken of using a rod and reel, more blue fish are taken on a hand line which, especially "outside" is far more easily managed. It is what we generally use, but those who prefer more science and fewer fish can use the more elegant tackle.

SPANISH MACKEREL.—These splendid fish which have become quite abundant at times on our coast of late years, are shy and difficult to capture. They were occasionally taken while trolling for blue fish, but we have sailed through miles of them and scarcely induced a half dozen to bite at the artificial squid. Persons have devoted their special attention to finding some line that would satisfy their dainty views, but with only moderate and partial success. They are wonderfully active and powerful, leaping from the water in long graceful curves like the mythical fishes of "Fairyland" and not like trout, salmon and blue fish, which either makes a quick snap or splash on the surface of the water, or jump a short distance out and up above it, falling back on the tails or sides, as often as on their heads. But the Spanish Mackerel pursue their prey, the small bony fish or mossbunkers and the spearing, with such velocity, that they throw themselves in a long arc out of water, when the latter rush to the surface and leap from it in their frantic efforts to escape. By this peculiarity, they can be distinguished from their coarser brethren the blue fish, and may be followed with the sail boat. On the South coast of Long Island, we have seen them "breaking in this way over miles square of water and have sailed by millions of them. The most successful troll is a squid made of red bone and with this as many as a hundred have occasionally been caught by the anglers being on the ground or rather water early in the morning. This red bone has a hook run through it in the ordinary way, and it is trolled behind a sail boat precisely in the same manner that blue fish are trolled. They are probably the finest fish for the table that are drawn from the salt or the fresh water and they are worthy of all the labor and patience required to catch them.

WEAK-FISH AND KING-FISH.—The latter of these are exceedingly the better fish to eat, and are deserving of the angler's attention whenever they can be found, which is only in a few of the salt water bays or inlets of our coast. They both take clam bait and the weak-fish will often take a white-fly fastened to the line above the bait, and used in bait-fishing not fly-fishing. King-fish are essentially bottom fish, and have a small sucker-like mouth, which can only swallow a small hook and bait; they are found on oyster beds which they no doubt explore for food. Once hooked, although they pull hard, they can rarely escape on account of the leathery nature of their lips unless the hooks break. They must be fished for close to the bottom. Many persons use a sinker on the end of the line with the hook or gut leader fastened six inches above, but we prefer a float and sinker and two hooks on leaders below the latter. By this rig, more space can be covered. Weak-fish, on the other hand, are mid-water fish, and have large mouths and soft jaws. For them, it is well to use a large Carlyle hook of fine steel with a round bend, a float and sinker, with but a short distance between them, and fine leaders of gut. Both of these fish like shedder crab, and at times will take the belly or soft part of the clam, when they will refuse the tougher portion usually used. The king-fish is always and everywhere rather scarce, but the weak-fish, was once taken in New York harbor in immense numbers and is so taken in Barnegat Bay. The first of flood tide, is usually preferred as the time for catching all salt water fish, but this is not a universal rule and often they will only bite on the first of the ebb, but if they bite on neither, it is useless to fish "between times."

CHAPTER XVII.

NETS AND NETTING.

Before closing this work we will say a few words concerning nets and the dangers that follow unrestricted net fishing. When the country was sparsely populated, and fish were abundant, the most ready and effectual methods of capturing them were the best. Now that all kinds of fish have become scarce, and some have disappeared altogether, limits must be placed on their destruction, and the kinds of nets and sizes of mesh must be regulated, or the supply will soon be utterly exhausted. There are strong and blindly selfish interests opposed to all legislation in such direction, but the public welfare is paramount and must prevail. If we are to have fish much longer abundant with us the use of nets must be regulated by law. Of all nets the most fatal are the pounds.

Pound nets are so called from a sort of trap or pound made of netting at their outermost extremity, so arranged that fish can enter it, but cannot escape. To this trap is attached a long wing or wall of netting, and it has mesh fine enough to prevent the passage of the smallest fish which are only used and only fit for manure, the mesh not being over one and a quarter inches stretched, or three quarters of an inch between knots. The wing reaches from the trap, which is either located in the channel or adjacent to it, well up ashore, and is hung on stakes driven firmly into the ground. It is sometimes six miles long, and has sometimes six traps at intervals of a mile each, and is never taken up after once it is set, except for a change of location, or old boreas removes them without permission of the owners. The plan of operation is this; A school of fish, or a single individual running into a harbor —for it is such localities that are usually selected —strikes against the wing, and is arrested in his course. Sometimes he turns back and goes to sea again. Timid fishes are often driven off in this manner, and never return, doing no good to the pound fishermen, nor to those who might have captured them in more legitimate ways. But if they are bold and determined they will push on, following the obstruction to its outer end, with the intention of passing around it. They are frequently of the class of migratory fishes which must change their element, and will strive by every means to overcome obstacles, or they may be shore varieties which are seeking some bay or shallow creek in which to spawn, and which it is very desirable should not be frustrated in their purpose. They swim cautiously, but perseveringly, along the wall of netting, but when they come to the end, instead of passing around it they are conducted into the trap, from which there is no escape, and where they await the arrival of the fisherman, who usually raises and empties his pound once or twice a day.

This simple statement of the plan of operation shows its great destructiveness. It is fishing all the while; day and night its victims are being led into the fatal traps. Nothing that comes along can escape, unless it be the timorous varieties, whose alarm carries them at once back to their haunts of safety and out of the reach of man. It is an inexpensive engine of piscatorial warfare as fatal to the masses of fish life as to the single individual voyaging alone. No one would object if there were fish enough for it and for the neighboring residents beside. Were that the case, it would be a convenient and effectual method of supplying the markets, but this is not the case, and while pound nets misappropriate the common stock, they overwork the fisheries, however prolific they may be, and in the end exhaust the supply. The more fish there are, the more are taken; none escape but the very few who follow the exact center of the channel. Not enough are left to keep up the breed, the habits of spawning are directly interfered with, the fishing begins to deteriorate, it never lasts but a few years, and at the close leaves that entire section of water absolutely bare of fish, dependent upon accident or the laborious efforts of man for its possible restoration.

Against this unfair appropriation of public property, the people have a manifest right to protest and legislate, and the question of investments of property in so glaring a wrong is not to be considered for a moment. The process has been permitted to go too far already, and the sooner it is stopped the more will be saved to the community. It has caused much harm, and is daily continuing its injurious work. In the New York Fishery reports reference has been made to many localities where the fishing, once excellent, was ruined by this process. The list can be extended every year.

Fallacious views have existed as to the migratory habits of fish. It has been supposed that they were accustomed to make long journeys, that they traveled up and down rivers, moved from shore to shore of broad lakes, and even crossed the ocean. The motions of anadromous fish had probably furnished ground for this opinion, but even as to them the impression is essentially incorrect. Shad appear first in the spring in the rivers of our southern states; as the season advances they begin to be taken in more northerly waters till in June and July they visit the streams of New England and then close their career,

Nothing was more natural than to suppose that these fish traversed the entire sea coast, coming in, perhaps, from the depths of the ocean or the warm waters of the Gulf of Mexico where they had been feeding during the winter, and gradually advancing northward as the hot days progressed, sending off a cohort into each river which was adapted to their propagation. Subsequent experiments have tended strongly to negative this theory as we have already explained and it is now believed among those best informed that fish move their quarters rarely and to only a limited extent; and that even migratory varieties remain not far from the mouths of the rivers which they ascend for the purposes of procreation.

The slow succession of changing varieties along our own coast confirm this later view of their habits. It is within the memory of man that the common blue-fish, *temnodon saltator*, arrived among us. It did not come all at once, but augmented slowly, displacing a coarser and larger variety of the mackerel family. But it had come to stay, and the advanced guard was soon joined by others.

It took up its permanent residence with us and proceeded to increase and multiply. It is now the most abundant of our salt water fishes. It stands at the head of the list and yet it may be on the way to displacement. We hope it is, as it is very voracious, and if supplanted at all will have a substitute its superior in every point. Within the last fifteen years the Spanish mackerel, *cybium maculatum*, has made its appearance among us. Taking its name from the Spanish West Indies where it was first only caught, it was wholly unknown on our shores till quite lately. Nor does it now seem to breed among us. The young are not found in any of our bays or creeks, but it is yearly becoming more and more numerous. Even now there are days in summer when the Long Island coast literally swarms with Spanish mackerel. They have been observed in solid schools twenty miles wide and of unknown length. These immense masses must evidently have come on from the south, but it has taken them years to get here. They have moved gradually and it is to be hoped they will be equally slow in leaving, and that they may supplant the blue-fish to which they bear a family resemblance. They are, as a table delicacy, the finest fish which is to be found in our country, and will add much to the attractions of our fish food if they remain with us.

This same unwillingness to change locality is still more observable among fresh water fish. The trout fisher has often observed a trout of unusual size occupying a certain spot in the stream, and expected always to find him until he was captured, or driven away. Salmon Trout and Pickerel fishing through the ice, in winter, demonstrates this love of locality in a still more marked degree. It is found that after fishing for a few days at one place, the fisherman can take no more, and he must move and cut new holes for his lines. Though it be only a change of a few hundred yards the fishing will be renewed and as good as ever. Now, if trout were in the habit of roaming about they would have no local habitation, but be taken in one part of the stream one day, and in another the next. So with Salmon Trout and pickerel, did they keep continually moving there would be no use in a fisherman changing his lines; he would only have to wait in one spot till the fish came round.

It is this peculiarity which rules in most if not all our fish which makes pound-netting so terribly destructive.

Was the supply at each favorable station continuously renewed from the vast storehouse of nature, it would make no difference if they were all fished out at any one particular spot—a short rest would recuperate the fishery and others would take the place of those which had been caught. As it is, however, when any locality is stripped clean and bare, it remains barren for a long time. Where only a few valuable fish are left, their natural enemies, being as numerous as ever, prevail against them and destroy the last remnant.

Possibly, after many years of waiting, strangers may work their way in; but it is a slow operation. If man endeavors to assist the process by artificial cultivation, he has nothing to work upon. He can get no eggs, because the parents are gone. He must import and plant new seed, an undertaking always difficult, and often doubtful.

Fykes are modified pound nets, and not so injurious unless too many of them are set, or the mesh is too small. They have short wing, and the outer end is kept open with hoops of wood, some being larger and some smaller, so as to make modified traps in which the fish are retained. The objection against them as they are now used is, that they catch the fry on account of the smallness of their mesh. Seines are sweep nets, and are the least injurious of all, as they give the fish a chance to slip by while they are not in use. Another destructive net is the gill net. It is used largely for shad, and is either attached to poles as a permanent and fixed fishing engine, or is floated by the current, suspended in the water.

Their length varies between one hundred and eight hundred fathoms. The largest of these require but one light skiff, with two, or at most, but three men to manage them. Being constructed of fine twine they are almost imperceptible to the fishes in the turbid tide waters. When later in the season the water becomes clear, greater execution is done by fishing at night. The mesh was formerly six and one-fourth inches, it is now reduced to five and even less, sufficiently large, however, to admit of the shad getting its head so far through the mesh that it is fastened by the gills, hence the term gill net, but so small as to take fish that should not be marketed.

These gill nets have both a lead and a cork line, by which they are held in a vertical position as they drift with the current. With the treble view of the economy of material, the prevention of injury by vessels of light draught in passing over them, and to enable the same net to be used with facility in either deep or shoal water, the upper margin of the net is supported by long and slender cords of from five to seven feet in length, to the free ends of which corks or wooden floats are attached. The net thus constructed is laid upon the stern of the skiff, one or two men, according to its size, row the boat across the current, while another standing on the stern carefully casts the net into the water. This done, it is suffered to drift with the tide, direction being given it by the boat to which the end remains attached. After the net has drifted a sufficient length of time, the fishes are removed from it, either by under-running it or by replacing it upon the stern of the boat, again to be cast into the water.

No nets should be used except in the ocean, the large rivers and lakes, and even then the mesh should be limited as to size, but as it is doubtful whether the community is ready for so sweeping a law, necessary as it is; the most injurious, which are the pound nets, should be everwhere prohibited. These are so fatal, that they should not be allowed anywhere unless it be in the ocean. We do not enter into any further details as to nets and net-fishing, for the reason that we are wholly opposed to their use except for two or three kinds of fish that can be taken in no other way and that are wholly food and not sporting fish. We believe that the sportsman and fish-culturist, has some rights which the net-fisherman is bound and will one day be made to respect. And the sooner that day comes the better for the community.

CONTENTS.

	PAGE.
INTRODUCTION	3
Chapter 1—Fish Culture	10
" 2—Trout Culture	19
" 3—Trout Ponds	30
" 4—Hatching House	38
" 5—Treatment of Eggs	50
" 6—Young Trout and Salmon	58
" 7—Adult Trout	74
" 8—Holton and other Hatching Boxes	93
" 9—Manipulating Salmon and Trout	102
" 10—General Remarks on Trout Breeding	121
" 11—Other Varieties of Fish	133
" 12—Shad Culture	141
" 13—Black Bass and other Fish	157
" 14—Fish Catching	176
" 15—Fishing for the Salmon Family	184
" 16—Fishing for Bass and other Fish	211
" 17—Nets and Netting	233

INDEX.

	PAGE.
American Waters	11
American Fish	13
Ainsworth's Screens	121
Alewives	156
Black Bass	13, 157, 159
Water	159
Spawning	159, 160
Young	159
Transportation	161
Fishing	211
Bullheads	see cat-fish
Brook Trout	see trout
Blue Swelling	69
Blind Fish	77, 87, 178
Bottom of Ponds	34, 38
Breeding of Trout	120
Semi-artificial	120
Bait-Fishing	208
Brewer's Fish Way	130
Blue-backed Trout	135
Bottom Fishing	223, 236
Blue Fish	226, 236
Trolling	227
Chumming	228
Cold Blooded Creatures	7
Connecticut River	12
Catfish	13, 158, 169
Carp	15, 157, 163
Commissioners of Fisheries	17
Cisco	13
Conferva	23
Cleanliness	61, 62
California Brook Trout	20, 64, 67, 86
Handling	67, 114
Cybium Maculatum	236
Chumming for Blue Fish	228
Cot	221
Casting the Fly	206
Casting Lines	see leaders
Changing Water in Cans of Fish	128
Cannibalism	89, 129
Cray-Fish	89

	PAGE.
Color of Fish	78
California Salmon	see Salmon, Cal.
Dry-Impregnation	16
Diseases	23, 68, 69, 87, 109
Diminution of Fish	25, 26, 144
Deformities	59
Distribution of Trout Fry	60
Enemies of Fish Life	22, 25, 54, 87, 90, 92
Eels	22, 93
Eggs when ripe	28, 111
How Fertilized	29, 111
Shells	37, 128
Number on Trays	42
Treatment	50
Placing in Troughs	50
Growth	53
Dead	53, 118
Transportation	54
Trays for	97
Inspecting	98
Loss of	106
Number in Fish	107
Washing	115
Wilmot's Treatment	117
Dead before impregnation	118
Killed by cold	119
Of Shad	155
Of Black Bass	160
Exhaustion of fisheries	238
Fish Culture, General Review	6
Compared with Agriculture	6, 7
Conclusions Established	9
Origin of	10
In American Waters	11
Foreign Method	15
Partly Natural Method	121
Palmer's Method	129
Fecundity	7
Fish Commissioners	17
Fish Catching	176
Fykes	238
Flies	193

	PAGE.
Filter	47
Feather Implement	49
Fry when Visible	53
Food of Trout Fry	63
Motion of	65
Food for Trout	79, 130
Salt	83
Fry of Shad	155
Fly-Fishing	184
for Striped Bass	222
For Shad	215
Fly Rods	184
Tying	193, 198
Book	197
Frog Culture	172
Fish Ways	131
Frozen Fish	119
Fungus	87, 109
Gold Fish	13, 92, 93, 158, 163
Government Aid	13
Grayling	20, 133
Spawns	20
Where found	134
Food	134
Gravel for troughs	48
Growth of Eggs	53
Trout, Salmon and Salmon Trout	66
Glass Trays	100
Jars	99
Gill Nets	238
Mesh	239
Hueninguen	13
Holton Hatching Box	16, 93, 139
Hatching Boxes	93
Coating	16
For Shad	16
Hatching House	38
of New York	39
Plan of	43
Herring	156
Hooks	197
Needle Point	198
Handling	108
Wilmot's Plan	117
Shad Eggs	152
Hearing in Fish	91
Hybrids	63, 168
Introduction	3
Impregnation	23, 111
Dry	16

	PAGE.
Impregnation—Percentage	29
After Death	118
of Whitefish	139
Implements for Fish Culture	49
Incubation of the Salmonidæ	23
Time of	52
Inspecting Eggs	98
Improving Streams	132
Jars of Glass for Trout Hatching	99
Kinds of Fish Cultivated	5, 7
King-fish	231
Lake Trout	see Salmon Trout
Lobsters	169
Propagation	171
Lines, for Trout and Salmon	190
Striped Bass	217
Leaders for Trout and Salmon	181, 191
Striped Bass	217
Localization of fish	237
Microscope	49
Measure	50
Moss for Transportation	54
Monstrosities	59
Maggots	65
Motion of Food	65
Muskrats	88
Minks	90
Manipulation of Salmon and Trout	102, 108, 112
of Shad	152
Milt	107, 110, 114, 115, 119
Migration of Salmon	20, 72
Shad	141
Fish	236
Migratory Fish confined to fresh water	154
Movement of embryo	165
Moths	194
Mascallonge	158
Fishing	213
New York Lakes	26
Commissioners	27
Nippers	49
Net for moving Trout	49, 108
Nursery for Trout Fry	59
Substitute for	62
Net from Worms	69
Night Fishing	181
Nets and Netting	238
Natural Spawning of Trout	103
Ova	see eggs

	PAGE.
Outfit for Fish Culture	122
Oswego Bass	158, 162
Fishing	213
Over-running of reels	221
Pike Perch	13, 14, 158, 162
Ponds for Trout	30, 60
Location	30
Laying out	31
Shape	31, 32
Raceways	32, 33
Bottom	34, 38
Holes through Banks	68
For Salmon	70
Pound Nets	233
Destructiveness	234
Preserving Fluid	174
Polywogs	173
Pickerel	158
Fishing	214
Price of Eggs and Fry	130
Palmer's Method of Fish Culture	129
Profit of Fish Culture	124
Pan for Spawn	110, 113
Plan of Hatching House	43
Proportion of Males and Females	107
Preserves	see Ponds
Rotation in Fish Culture	8
Rats	54
Remedies for Disease	87, 91
Raceway	32, 33, 108
Netting, from	108
Net for	108
Restripping Female Trout	114
Rock Bass	162
Rock-fish	see Striped Bass
Rods for Fly Fishing	184
Reels	205
Running Sinker	223
Success of Fish Culture	3
Suitable Varieties of Fish	13
Salmon Trout	13, 64, 66
Fishing	209
Trolling for	211
Salmon	13, 64
Culture	19
Rivers	19
Family Scientific Names	20
California	20, 64, 66, 70, 71, 77, 85
Migration	20, 72
Nests	20
Spawning	21, 77, 102

	PAGE.
Salmon—Eggs	21
Time in which Eggs Hatch	23
Young	58
Fry	58
Growth	66, 77
Land Locked	130
Confined to Fresh Water	154
Fishing	184
Rods	189
Flies	198
Seines	238
Smell of Fish	179
Scent of Fish	176
Strawberry Bass	158
Supply of Water	37, 38, 46, 74
Sediment	47, 96
Shipping Eggs	54
Starvation	69
Salt Food for Fish	83
Shading Ponds	85
Salt Water Bath for Disease	91
Syphon	97, 99
Self-picker	99
Spawning of Trout	21, 102, 103, 108
Salmon	21, 77, 102
Spanish Mackerel	230, 236
Shape of Ponds	31, 32
Skin of Trout Delicate	109
Stripping Fish	108
Seth Green taking Spawn	112
Spermatozoa	115
Stocking Ponds	122
Streams	123
Smelt	136
Screens	33, 60, 129
Cleaning	68
Ainsworth's	121
Salt Water Herring	156
Streams, how Improved	132
Sturgeon	164
Shad	13, 141
Trays	97
Habits	141
Migration	141
Natural Propagation	145
Natural Loss	146
Box	147
Artificial Culture	148
Errors in Fish Culture	148
Development of Egg	149
Distribution of Fry	150

	PAGE.
Shad—Handling the Eggs	152
Ponding the Parents	153
Confined to Fresh Water	154
Sent to California	155
Transportation of Eggs	155
Temperature	156
Acclimatization	155, 156
Fly-fishing	215
Striped Bass	158, 166
Spawning	167
Fishing	216
Lines for	217
with Menhaden	218
with Lobster	220
Fly-fishing	222
with Shrimp	223
with Crab	224
with Spearing	225
Trout	13, 97
Culture, general considerations	19, 120
California	20, 64, 67, 86
Nests	20
Spawning	21, 102
Eggs, 21	see eggs
of Rangeley	22, 75
Time of Incubation	23, 52
Fry	24, 58
Natural Hatching	25
Geographical Distribution	27
Young	58
Removal	60
Food	63, 79
Growth	66, 75, 76
Adult	74
Long Island	76
Waters for	86
Cannibals	89
Our practice in Hatching	100, 108
Crowding together	101
Netting	108
Culture Profitable	125
Blue-backed	135
Fishing	184

	PAGE.
Trout—Rods	189
Troughs for Trout	44
to Cleanse	61
Zinc	129
Temperature	27, 52, 84, 86
That will kill Eggs	119
for Shad	156
Treatment of Eggs	50
Time of Incubation	52
Tameness of Fish	83
Trays	97
of Glass	100
Number of Eggs on	42
Double in Trough	120
Baskets	163
Taking Spawn by Hand	108
Tiring out Fish	113
Transporting Live Fish	127
Times for	127
Number to each Can	128
Black Bass	161
Tackle	181
Trolling for Trout	208
Thumb-stall	221
Umbilical Sac	24
Wall-eyed Pike	see pike-perch
Whitefish	13, 20, 97
Hatching Box for	94
Eggs Impregnated after Death	118
Welcher's Treatment	138
Raising the Fry	139
Food for	140
Weak Fish	231
White Perch	158, 162
Welcher's Method with Whitefish	138
Wilmot's Handling	117
Washing Eggs	115
Water Snakes	89
Worms	69
Water Supply	37, 38, 46, 74
Wastefulness of Nature	22
Yellow Perch	13, 158
Fishing	214

www.ingramcontent.com/pod-product-compliance
Lightning Source LLC
Chambersburg PA
CBHW020805230426
43666CB00007B/867